GW00865392

Pages From Her Story

Pages From Her Story

Teresa Greer Drew

ISBN-13: 9781545249666
ISBN-10: 1545249660
Library of Congress Control Number: 2017905663
CreateSpace Independent Publishing Platform
North Charleston, South Carolina

Some names, identifying characteristics, and locations, have been changed in order to maintain their anonymity.

Scriptures quoted are from the New American Standard Bible (NASB). When any other version is used, I've indicated it in the text.

Every person's life is a fairy tale
written by God's fingers.

—Hans Christian Andersen

For Betty Ann

Thank you, Betty Ann, for entering into my life and showing me Jesus. My hope in sharing *Pages From Her Story* is to enter into the lives of others and do the same.

Contents

Preface

Pages From Her Story is a collection of stories about the transformation of a woman whose heart was broken but brought back to life when she met God. It is about the story God tells us in all our lives. It is about humanity and the world and how an awareness of God changes and infuses everything, making a difference in our everyday life. It is the snapshots of a woman learning to be everything she was created to be and participating with God in His mission in this world.

These stories are about love, redemption, hope, forgiveness, trust, and reconciliation. As you read—the broken parts, the secret parts, and the beautiful parts—the gospel will come to life. That's the transforming story of what God does in a human heart. It can come alive, and that story can change your life.

There Is a Purpose for Your Life

I was sitting on the ground, looking up at an old wooden cross hanging on the side of a tree. It felt like someone was with me, but I couldn't see anyone. Somehow I knew I was OK. I knew there was a purpose for my life.

When had it all started? When my childhood sweetheart, told me he was confused and didn't think he wanted to be married any longer. At first, I just wanted to help him any way I could. He needed time; he needed a place to think and, maybe, pray. He asked me if I would go stay with my family for a short while so he could be alone and think through some things. Of course, I would; I would do whatever he needed for me to do. He would be OK.

It was sometime in the autumn, you know; I can't remember exactly the time or the day, but it was near Christmas. He would be OK by Christmas, and we would have a great holiday. I would call him, check on him, and see if he was OK. I would even go by and check on the house, straighten up and clean.

One day, very near to Christmas, as I said I can't remember the days exactly, I went over to check on him and see if the house needed cleaning. As I drove down the road toward the house, something was not right. He told me he had to go out of town for a short time—business, he said; that is why I chose this time. I would clean the house for him, thus surprising him. His car was in the driveway. I pulled in behind him. I knew something was not right. I went up to the door, unlocked it, and walked in.

The house was dark, but there was some vague light back toward the bedroom. I walked in the living room first. There were some articles there that I didn't recognize—clothes, a purse, and shoes; it looked like presents just opened. I turned and went into the kitchen. Someone had been cooking; the table was full of dishes—two plates, wineglasses, and utensils, and there were candles still burning.

Wineglasses? My husband didn't drink. He had always been against drinking alcohol; many times I had asked him if we could celebrate with a glass of wine just for a special occasion—it would be so much fun. He would say, "No, it is not good for us; it is a sin." But there on the table were two glasses half-full with red wine.

I walked over to the kitchen area. There was a half-eaten casserole of mushrooms. My husband hated mushrooms, or that is what he always told me. Why was he eating mushrooms?

I turned and walked down the hall, stopped at the bathroom, and turned on the light. The tub was half-full of water with bubble bath. On the side of the tub were two more glasses of wine. There were more clothes on the floor. I turned and walked out.

I started down the hallway again. I could hear noises. Even as I stood there, I don't know if it registered with me exactly what was going on. I was so confused. No, not my husband…I had known him since I was fifteen. He was everything to me. He loved me; we loved each other. We had promised to be together forever.

As I started toward the doorknob, he came out of the room and closed the door. I remember looking at him with such confusion, hurt, and pain. He touched me and tried to direct me back to the living room. I jerked away from him, told him not to touch me, not to ever touch me.

He tried to talk to me, but I didn't know what he was saying. I was surrounded with a pain I had never, ever known my whole life. I am not even sure I would call it pain. Pain was when I stumped my toe. This was an agonizing hurt in my chest that I didn't know how to describe. I couldn't even see clearly. I believe we were standing in the living room, and I told him to get her out of my house, out of my bed. He kept trying to talk to me, but I couldn't hear him. I kept saying, "Get out of my house now!" I believe he even got upset with me, wanted me to leave, give him some time, and come back later.

I screamed for him to get her out of my house. He left me standing there and went back to the bedroom. I turned and sat in a chair. I didn't want to see her or him. I am not sure how long I sat there, but I remember hearing a noise and the door open and close.

I really don't remember anything else until days later, but this is what my mother, sister, and brother-in-law told me. I called my mother and told her where I was. She said she didn't even recognize her daughter's voice and knew something was terribly wrong. She sent my brother-in-law to the house to get me. He told me I was sitting in the middle of the living-room floor with tears running down my face and that I couldn't speak. He said I acted as though I didn't know where I was or what was going on. He helped me to the car and took me to my mom's.

Mom tells me that for the next four days, I lay in the bed, would not get up, would not eat, would not do anything, and that I cried. She says she didn't know what to do with me and was so scared.

I don't remember any of this. The first thing I remember was sitting beside my bed one morning and crying so hard I couldn't see. I remember that terrible pain in my chest, and I lay face down on the floor. I remember Mom coming in and begging me to get up and to stop crying. I couldn't even talk to her.

I got up and went to my car. I do not know where my family was when I did this, but I got into my car and started driving. I didn't know where I was going, but I knew it was a good time to die. I didn't think I could do something to myself, but maybe I would have a wreck; maybe I would drive over a cliff. I hoped something like this would happen. I remember saying, "Lord, this would be a good time for you to take me." I didn't really know if He was there or not, but I remember saying those words over and over.

I never knew how long I drove that day; maybe around four hours, but that is just a guess. I remember pulling my car over to the side of the road, getting out and walking up an incline and into the forest. I remember feeling absolutely nothing inside, but the forest seemed like the right place to go. I kept walking.

I don't know how long I walked that day, either, but I remember walking into a clearing, falling on the ground and crying out to God. You see, I had professed to know God since I was fourteen years old.

I accepted Christ at a Billy Graham crusade. It was the first time I had heard that God loved me, and I was compelled to walk down to the front and receive what this man was talking about. But now was different; the man I loved was gone. I didn't know anything else.

Once again, I have no idea how long I lay on that ground crying. I continued to cry out to a God Whom I didn't know; don't we all do that? When our life falls apart, we say God's name over and over. Why do we do that? Do we believe in Him or do we not?

As I was lying there and finally stopped crying, I thought someone walked up. It felt so strong to me that I looked up. I sat up and looked around me. I didn't see anyone, but then I looked up. What was that? At the top of a tree was an old, large wooden cross. I kept looking at it. Why was it there? I stared at it, and again I have no idea how long, but deep down somewhere, I knew this cross was for me. I knew there was a purpose for me, even with what had happened.

I got up and started walking again. Something was different. I didn't know what it was or exactly what had just happened to me, but I knew I was going to be OK. The pain was still there, but it wasn't crushing me. I walked and actually looked around me. The place was very pretty. I hadn't even seen it before. I don't remember seeing anything in days; there were flowers everywhere, the sun was shining, and it felt warm outside.

I heard a dog barking. I looked around to see where it was. I saw this large black dog running toward me from across the meadow. For some reason I wasn't scared; I just watched him. He came close and stopped about two feet from me. He continued to bark. He looked at me, and I looked at him. Even though he started to growl, and I could see the large white teeth, I wasn't scared. Standing there that day, I knew this dog was like the world; it could be a hard, cruel, and scary place, but I was safe. I didn't know how or why, but I had a peace I had never known before or understood.

I walked away; the dog ran back to where it came from. I came out of the forest and saw my car on the side of the road. I got into it and drove home. I knew Mom would be worried.

I had left the house that day hoping to die. I was twenty-four years old and knew that life was over for me. I kept calling out to a God, not believing

He was there or could or would ever help me. I thought I knew the answer. I thought I knew what should happen to me. I wanted to die, but I met God that day.

The place I ended up that day was a Baptist camp. Of all the places in the world, I ended up in a Baptist camp. Why? God had a plan. I knew I had a purpose that day. Even when the person I thought was life itself walked away, when the life I knew had been destroyed, when I knew the only answer was death, God met me.

We have a Creator Who created us for a purpose, and when we think that life itself is over, He shows us who we really are and what we mean to Him. He cares about humanity; He cares about us intimately. He took me to a Baptist camp and showed me the cross.

There is purpose to our lives.

Do you understand that no matter what has happened to you, where you have been, or what you have done, God is there; He will meet you.

It's in Christ that we find out who we are and what we are living for. Long before we first heard of Christ and got our hope up, he had his eye on us, had designs on us for glorious living, part of the overall purpose he is working out in everything and everyone.

—EPHESIANS 1:11, THE MESSAGE

Forgiveness

I walked out the door. It slammed. I couldn't believe she said that to me. I have to forgive him? He was the one who had lied, he was the one who had been unfaithful, I had found him with another woman, and my mom was telling me to forgive him! That was crazy! I walked down the driveway, got into my car, and left the house.

—⁂—

I had known Bethany for a couple of years. She worked part time in the pediatrician office I worked in—the place where I had gone to when I thought it would help my marriage if I stopped working so many hours and spent more time with my husband. I talked to her a little bit but didn't really know her.

When we separated, I realized I needed more money, so I got a job in the operating room in the hospital. I was leaving the pediatrician office. I would miss the girls; we had all become very close. On my last day, they had a party for me. Bethany was there. As I was saying good-bye to everyone, Bethany came up to me, gave me a hug, and put something into my uniform pocket. She whispered in my ear that it was her phone number, asking me to call her if I ever needed her and not to hesitate. What? I hardly knew her. I would never call her.

I was working in the operating room one day. Because this was a specialty, and I was new, I was assigned to work with another registered nurse. The lady I was working with scared me a little bit. She had a very strong personality and was very outspoken. On this particular day, I could not think clearly. I had been out of work for about two weeks. You see, a few weeks before, I had walked into my house and discovered my husband with another woman. I was devastated and, for the past few weeks, had been in bed, not able to get up. I really couldn't believe the hospital had not fired me; they had not. But what was I going to do? I couldn't think clearly. I just kept seeing the picture of my husband with this woman.

I was helping the doctor with a patient; he was talking to me, but I couldn't hear him. His mouth was moving, but I just couldn't hear what he was saying. Finally the doctor yelled to get me out of the room. The nurse I was working with escorted me out of the room quickly. She took me to a closet, put me in a chair, and told me not to move.

I have no idea how long I sat there. My mentor came into the closet, sat down beside me, and told me to look at her. Her words penetrated through the haze of pain. She said, "Teresa, I don't know what you are going through. I know it must be painful. I can see it on your face. But I am here to tell you right now that if you don't get it together, you will be fired. I don't want to see that happen; you are a good nurse." She told me to go home for the rest of the day.

I wandered up to the front of the operating-room section of the hospital. What was I going to do? I could lose my job? How would I live? I remember wringing my hands together, being agonized with this haze of pain all around me. I put my hands in the pocket of my uniform. I felt something and pulled it out of my pocket. It was a piece of paper, and it had something on it. I tried to read it but couldn't quite make it out. I looked closer. It was Bethany's phone number. How many times had I washed this uniform?

I found a phone. I picked up the receiver, stared at the number, and dialed. Why was I doing this? A woman's voice answered. I do not know exactly what I said to her. She told me years later that I was crying, telling her I didn't know why I was calling her, but that I didn't know what I was going to do. Bethany asked me where I was. I told her the hospital. She asked when I would finish work. I told her they told me to leave now. She asked me to come over.

I don't remember driving to her house, but I got there. I walked up to her door and knocked. This lady opened the door and let me in. She hugged me, and I cried. She took me to a large, cozy chair by the window and sat me down, and I cried. She sat beside me in another large, cozy chair. She let me cry. After a while, she got up and made tea.

She didn't ask me any questions that day; she just took care of me physically and let me grieve. I continued to go see Bethany. I was drawn to her. I felt such peace with her and in her house, in that big chair by the window. What was it about her? She looked so peaceful, and she smiled.

One day I asked her about it. She talked to me about Jesus. I told her I had accepted Christ when I was fourteen but never knew Who He was. I didn't understand what she had; could she tell me more?

She was happy to. I went to her house every day after I left the hospital. She welcomed me, let me sit in the cozy chair, offered me all kinds of food, and told me about Jesus. She would read to me from the Bible.

One day I asked her, "How do I get rid of this terrible pain that makes my chest hurt? Will it ever go away?" This is the day she told me about forgiveness. This is the day I stormed out of her house.

How was this possible? My husband had been the one who had left our marriage, he was the one seeing another woman, and he was the one who had said he didn't love me anymore; what did Bethany mean I had to forgive him?

I had been reading the Bible a little. Bethany told me it was Jesus's words. It was a letter to us, and it was how we were to live. One night, after I had been angry for days, I walked around the house thinking about Bethany's words: "Teresa, the only way you will be free is to forgive your husband and release him to God." I found my Bible. It was so new, I could hardly turn the pages. I got up in the middle of my bed; I was going to find in this Bible where Jesus said you did not have to forgive a man who had hurt a woman, the way my husband had hurt me. I knew it had to be there. I searched and searched—all night.

It was around three in the morning, and I remember crying out to God, still not really sure where He was, "It has to be here. What do you mean about this forgiveness? I was the one hurt. I am still hurting. He is running around doing whatever he wants to do. God, help me understand."

I opened my Bible to Matthew, and I saw where this disciple, Peter, asked Jesus how many times he had to forgive his brother—up to seven times? Jesus actually said to him, "I do not say to you seven times, but up to seventy times seven" (Matthew. 8:21–35). And He always said, "Forgive."

What? I just couldn't find where Jesus said it was OK not to forgive your husband when he lied to you, betrayed you, broke a covenant with you, rejected you, and hurt you beyond any pain you had ever known.

I had to go see Bethany. Would she let me come over again? I had not been very nice. I had left without saying good-bye. She was my only hope. The next afternoon, when I left the hospital, I drove to her house; very slowly, I parked the car and went up to the door. I was afraid she would ask me to leave, but she opened the door, gave me a big hug, and escorted me to my favorite chair by the window. She made tea and asked if I wanted something to eat.

Who was this woman? I didn't know it at the time, but she reflected the character of her Savior to me. I was drawn to her and wanted to know more about this Jesus and what He had to say about forgiveness.

I think one of the most amazing things she said to me that day was that forgiving someone was not saying what the other person did was OK. It was saying that what you did to me hurt; it made me feel this way or that way; I didn't like it, and I am angry with you. But I am going to make a choice, by the act of my will, to forgive you, because it is what Jesus tells me do. It is what He did with me. I trust you, God, to work this out in me, to make it a reality, to give me the mind of Christ, to heal my damaged emotions and line them up with the truth I choose to believe. Bethany told me that I might not understand it right then, but there was an enemy of my soul, and he did not want me to live in freedom, that he would remind me over and over of the incident, but I was to give it right away to Jesus. She told me to memorize some scripture and repeat it over and over when these thoughts or the picture came to mind.

The next day I was running an operating room with five cases. That meant five patients I had to take care of, five sets of scrub nurses, five sets of doctors, and five sets of anesthesiologists; I was dealing with life and death, moment by moment. I believe that day the thoughts and picture of my husband with another woman came to my mind five thousand times. Each time, I would say I have forgiven, I give this to Jesus, and I would quote a scripture. The scripture I had memorized was from Philippians 4:6-8, *Be anxious for nothing, but in everything by prayer and supplication with thanksgiving let your requests be made known to God. And the peace of God, which surpasses all comprehension, will guard your hearts and your minds in Christ Jesus. Finally, brethren, whatever is true, whatever is honorable, whatever is right, whatever is pure, whatever is lovely, whatever is of good repute, if there is any excellence and if anything worthy of praise, dwell on these things.*

I remember once a doctor asked me what I was saying. It was constant that day and many days after this. I am not sure exactly when it was, but I didn't have to do it so much anymore; the picture was less and less. I can describe it like a giant hole in my heart and someway, somehow, God filled it up with, I guess, His peace, love, grace, and mercy. I am not saying I forgot, but the pain and the emotion was not so agonizing; my heart didn't hurt as much as before.

I remember the last time I saw my husband, I told him I forgave him. He looked at me and asked how I could even look at him, much less forgive him. I told him the only way I knew was God. I want to dedicate what I have just written to this lady, Bethany. God brought her in my life and ministered to me through her. She is a picture of Jesus; her obedience to God and her love, care, and sacrificing of herself saved my life. You see, if I had not forgiven my husband, I would still be in bondage to him. He would still be controlling me. I would not have been able to walk down a different path with God.

Our lives make a difference. Bethany's made a difference. Thank you, my sweet friend.

Is there anyone you need to forgive today? Release them and release yourself. Jesus came so we can walk in freedom. Forgiveness is freedom.

Hearing God

I met God when my husband left me. I had heard about God all my life, from the time I was a little girl. But I had associated God with a monster. I thought He lived in this place called heaven (I had no idea where or what this was) and sat in a big chair, watching me. When I did something wrong, He would get me. I can't really tell you how I thought He did this, but He did.

My parents went to church when I was young. I learned much about God from this church. The man up front in a place called a pulpit yelled a lot. He often talked about hell, fire, and brimstone, whatever that was. He even told us we were going there if we didn't watch out. I always felt fear. I was so scared I would do something wrong and this monster called God would get me.

At night I couldn't go to sleep. I had to have a light on. If I slept through the night, the next night I would wonder, *How did I hold my legs last night? Did I cross them? Did I lie on my back or my side?* And then I would try to lie the same way, hoping I would sleep that night. I believe that is called magical thinking.

I was always watching everything I did, because I didn't want this monster to get me. I always obeyed my parents because that man up front in the church told me I would go to hell if I didn't. If there was ever anything I didn't think my parents would like, I wouldn't tell them, or I would make it sound better, because I didn't want them to get upset. If they got upset, this monster called God would get upset.

When I was fourteen, I went with my youth group to listen to this man named Billy Graham speak. Oh, he started talking about God, but he didn't yell. I didn't even hear the words "hell," "fire," or "brimstone." He said God loved me. What? I can't remember everything he said, but I do remember that when he finished, I had to go down to the front, where he was inviting us to come. He asked us if we wanted to invite Jesus to come into our hearts. I knew I wanted the peace and love that radiated from this man's face. He told us to ask God for forgiveness and to ask Jesus to come into our hearts. Well, I knew all about sins; I was always doing something wrong and messing up, so I could do this.

I did. I asked Jesus to come into my heart. Now I had no idea what all this meant, but I believe that even though I didn't know, God knew, and He heard me. I believe I became a Christian at that time. I started going to church where this cute boy from school went. I wanted to meet him. This church didn't talk much about Jesus, though. They talked about what was happening in the world and how to be a nice person.

The cute boy turned out to be a jerk, but I met another boy who was nice. We started dating when I was sixteen. We were together all the time. I didn't hear much about Jesus in this church or anywhere else, but I was in love.

It was a good thing I had met this guy, because my parents were not getting along very well, and I didn't like to be at home. My parents eventually separated. They went back to the church we went to when I was very young. They didn't stay long; because that man who spoke from the pulpit told them they were going to hell if they divorce. They divorced and were very unhappy.

I was very sad for my parents, but I had met this guy. We continued going to this church. I don't remember learning very much about Jesus, but this boy and I got closer and closer. All I really remember them saying about Jesus was that His teachings from the Bible was for two thousand years ago, not for today. I always thought that was a bit funny. There was a plaque right behind the minister's head that read, *Jesus is the same yesterday, today and forevermore* (Heb. 13:8). But I thought since this guy was the pastor and went to some school, he must know. And there were many people sitting in the church listening, so it must be true. This boy and I dated all through high school and then into college. We were going to get married. I even went to school through the summers so we could get married in three years' time instead of four.

Once I graduated from college, we married. We bought a house and had many plans for our life. We were going to wait around five years and then start a family. We had it all figured out, that big thing called life.

When I was twenty-four, my husband told me he was confused and didn't think he wanted to be married any longer. We ended up separating, and I found out there was another woman in his life.

The last ten years I had learned a lot about this boy, but I had not learned anything about Jesus. I called Him Savior at age fourteen but didn't know anything about Him. This lady I know today was brought into my life by my Creator; she taught me about Jesus, she showed me Jesus.

One of the things she told me was that Jesus still spoke today. He still guided and directed us today. He created us, you might say; He designed us because He loved us. His Word was not just for two thousand years ago, and He was not a monster.

I remember the first time I knew God spoke to me. I was in my apartment, the place I was living while my husband and I were separated. It was a cozy little place. I liked it. I was in my bathroom combing my hair. I had been trying to make the decision whether to continue seeing a counselor whom someone had recommended to me. I had seen him once; he just sat there and listened to me, not saying a word. I was not at peace about seeing this man. I tried to pray, but I wasn't sure how. I just kept saying, "God, help me; God show me." That is all I really knew how to do when it came to praying. I still struggled with my feelings of fear when it came to God. I knew in my head that He was not a monster; at least that was what I was learning, but not in my experience. I still felt like that little girl who was afraid of God and knew He was going to get me if I did anything wrong or something He didn't like. But as I stood there combing my hair, I heard these words, "Teresa, I am your Counselor." I turned around, poked my head out the door of the bathroom, and looked down the hallway. I walked into the living room, kitchen, and then my bedroom. I knew someone was in the apartment. I didn't see anyone. I went back into the bathroom and stood looking at myself in the mirror. Who or what was that? Could that be God?

I called the lady who was teaching me, told her what happened, and asked if she thought that could be God. She gave me a scripture. I looked it up. I couldn't believe it. The words were in the Bible! God was saying to me that He would be my counselor.

I didn't see the other counselor again. God made a promise to me that day, and He has never let me down. He has truly been a Counselor to me. I was so amazed. God is the same yesterday, today, and forevermore. He is alive today, not just two thousand years ago. Wow!

I remember another time I heard God. I believe when you are just meeting your Heavenly Father, He gives so much grace and makes it a little easier for you. I don't always hear God like this today, but He was showing Himself to a scared little girl that He was alive, that He cared, and that He was not a monster. Today, most of the time, it is just this deep-down knowing or an impression through His Word.

I was driving home from a friend's house. I was going to be driving right past where my husband was living. I had this knowing that I was to stop and tell him I forgave him, that I had met God and He was not like what we thought, and I knew He could put our marriage together again if we let Him. I remember thinking, *This is crazy! I can't do that.* Oh, but it was so strong. I had been learning about God, and one of the things I was learning was that when you hear Him, obey Him.

I stopped and told my husband. He just looked at me. I knew he thought I was crazy. Do you know what? God had me do that two more times! I remember after the third time and my husband still told me no; I was mad at God. Why did He have me to do this? Did I not hear Him right? Was I crazy? How humiliating. And he was the one who left me!

I didn't understand any of it until one day about eight months after my divorce. I was standing at the ironing board in the same apartment where I had been living. I was planning to meet a young man. I was ironing a shirt. I didn't want to go and meet this man. Wasn't this a little like dating? I didn't want to date. I knew I was divorced, but, oh, I still felt married. Was this the right thing? God didn't like divorce. I was torn.

I prayed. Praying was still a little hard for me. I wasn't sure how to do it. But you know what I know today? It may have been hard for me, but God heard me. He knew my heart. He knew I didn't know how, but He listened and He answered. I sensed these words so strongly: "That is why I had you to go back to your husband and ask three times for reconciliation, to tell him the truth about me. He said no. Now I will take you down a different path. I could have healed your marriage, but it was a choice. Now let's go down this path." I knew in my heart it was OK to let go, to move forward, to look ahead, and to trust God. I didn't know what lay ahead, but I knew Who was with me. I knew He was alive, and I knew He was not a monster.

I am still learning about hearing God's voice, obeying and following what He says. It has been an adventure—an amazing one! Sometime it is hard and usually always goes against what the world tells us to do. Would the world tell you to forgive and try to put your marriage back together when your husband left you for another woman? I don't think so. I am so glad I obeyed God. I don't think I would be in the same place today if I had not.

> *It's urgent that you get this right: The time has arrived—I*
> *mean right now!—when dead men and women will hear the*
> *voice of the Son of God and hearing will come alive.*

—JOHN 5:25–27

Dependency

I couldn't believe I was about to do this. I walked into the gas station. A man sitting on a stool jumped up and asked if he could help me. I was about to cry. I said to the man, "I know this is a self-serve gas station, and I will be happy to self-serve, but I don't know how. If you can show me how to do it, I promise I will always come to this station and self-serve in the future." He stared at me. He kind of laughed but said, "Come on." He walked to the door, opened it, let me out first, and we walked to the pumps. He was so nice. He showed me how to put gas in my car. My husband always told me self-serve was the best way to go. I told the man what my husband had said. He agreed. I learned how to put gas in my car, and I always went to that gas station from day on.

I didn't know how to write a check. I had to open an account. My husband and I were separated, and I had to have my own bank account. I walked into the bank. It was a bit intimidating; everyone looked so important. I walked over to a desk where this lady sat. She asked what I wanted and invited me to take a chair. I waited for about twenty minutes. I was nervous. Finally this man stepped out of an office and invited me inside. I sat down in another chair. He said, "I understand you want to open an account?" I told him I had never been inside a bank. I was twenty-four then. He stared at me for a moment and then said, "Well, let me show you how we open this account." Thank you, God.

I had lived in one city all my life. It was a very small city in North Carolina. It was a beautiful place; I thought it was the only place in the world. I had a friend who lived in Virginia. She invited me to visit with her. That sounded so nice to me. I needed to spend some time with her. She called to give me directions to her house. She started at some highway north of where I lived. I interrupted her as she was talking and said, "I need for you to start from my driveway. I have never left this town and don't know how to get to the highway." There was silence. After a few minutes, she said, "Sure, let's start at the beginning." I was so thankful.

It was the end of the year. Someone told me I had to file taxes and that if I didn't, I could go to jail. How was I to do that? I discovered that an accountant could do them. I drove up Main Street, looking for an accountant. There was a signboard with the name of the accountant written on it. I parked the car in front of the building, gathered together all the necessary papers from my front seat, and put it in a big yellow envelope. The papers were sticking out everywhere. I walked into the office. I waited for a while; finally the secretary told me I could go into this office. I walked in with this big yellow envelope in my hands. A man looked up from his desk. I knew I was about to cry. He asked if he could help me. I walked over to his desk, dropped the yellow envelope on top of it, and all the papers flew everywhere. I said, "I understand I need to file tax returns, but I don't know how. I don't even understand what I was supposed to bring to you, but here is a bunch of stuff. I am sorry to be so much trouble, but can you please help me?" He stared at me for a few minutes and then reached over to the telecom, spoke to his secretary, and cancelled his afternoon appointments. He told me to sit down. This man helped me for over five hours that day. He told me many years later that he could not get over the look on my face, and something deep inside him told him to help me. Thank you, God, and thanks to this man.

When my husband had left me, I didn't know what to do. I had been with him since I was fifteen, and I had become very dependent on him for everything! I was dependent on him physically, emotionally, and mentally. I didn't know how to do even the simplest things for myself.

Shortly after the separation, I met God. He was taking me down a different path than the one I thought I was going to walk down in life. God had some things to show me as we walked down this path.

God showed me many of the things that I looked to my husband for, which my husband was never to meet. We are all created to be with God; He loves, accepts, and values us. Jesus entered into our world to rescue us, to rescue humanity. My husband had a lot of responsibility, more than he was meant to have.

God created us; He knows how we work the best. He will work through people in our lives to meet our needs, but we must seek Him first and trust Him. We need to lay down all the ways we have tried to meet those needs. It was so hard for me to trust God when my husband left. I had always looked to him for approval; he told me if I was OK. But God had already said in His word that when I was not OK, He entered into our world and met me, us. Because of Jesus, I now had God's approval, and I didn't need to get that constantly through my husband.

Oh, it didn't feel right, though. It felt so wrong. I knew my worth was in my husband and what he thought of me, and now that he was gone, there was nothing. But that was not what God's Word said to me. He said that I was His child, that He loved, accepted, and valued me. I would keep reading His Word, trying to understand. Someone finally told me that if I waited till I felt like it, I would never do it. I needed to make a choice. That word "choice"…I never really thought of myself having a choice with anything. I always look to other people to tell me what to do. But God was telling me to make a choice and then He would deal with my feelings.

I made that choice. Sometime I made it over and over, a thousand times a day. Every time my feelings said no, I would make that choice again. I would say, "God, I choose to believe you, regardless of what I feel." It was such baby steps at first, but I was depending on God. I was trusting God

God was helping me so much. He was with me, even when I did not realize it. As I look back on all these times of learning how to do things—putting gas in my car, writing a check, driving and handling taxes, and so on—God was there. I didn't feel it at that time; I was scared, but look at even the people He put in my life—He has showed grace.

Today I am much more aware of God, and I have come a long way in my journey with Him, but it is still moment-by-moment with Him. I can't do it the way I always did it in the past. Oh, I wish sometime I could put together a formula from my early years and then follow it all throughout my life, but would that be dependency on God or dependency on the formula? I think you know the answer!

As I look through the Bible, the only pattern, formula I see is dependency on God—looking to Him in each situation, hearing His voice and obeying.

Are you looking for a formula? Yes, it would be easier, but walk your life with God, participating with Him in the moment. Ask Him to help you be so aware of His presence with you at all times.

No, I could not trust my emotions in the beginning, but God has brought much healing, and so many times He now leads me by my desires.

But we are to always…

> *Seek first His kingdom and His righteousness, and all these things will be added to you.*
>
> —MATTHEW 6:33

Trust

I was sitting at the back of the airplane with my instructor. We had just taken off. I couldn't believe it; I was flying! I looked out the window, and there were the clouds; they were right beside us! I looked over at my instructor; she was sitting beside me. She saw the awe on my face and finally asked the question, "You have never flown before, have you?" I had not wanted to tell her, but I couldn't help myself. I said, "No, I haven't; this is amazing! I have never seen anything like it."

She stared a bit longer and then laughed. She said, "I can't believe that someone applied to be a flight attendant and had never flown before!" She asked if I was OK, whether I had any motion sickness. I said, "Absolutely not."

I was on an airline, and a group of us were having our first practice trip. In just a few minutes, we were going to take the cart up the aisle and offer drinks and peanuts. I was so thankful and couldn't believe I was doing what I was doing. I was about to become a flight attendant. I had two more weeks of training to complete, and then I was moving to Washington, DC. I was going to be based out of an airport there. Washington, DC, can you believe that? I was a little girl who had never left a small town in North Carolina and then living in a big city like DC I was in awe.

I had been working in the operating room as a registered nurse for a couple of years. I loved the job and the people, but I had a desire to travel, to see the world. Well, first I wanted to see the United States, but the hospital was short of nurses; they would not let me have any time off. I had asked for a six-month leave of absence; they thought I was crazy.

I was growing in my relationship with God. My husband and I had been divorced for a couple of years now. Even though I told him I had met someone Who could put our marriage back together if we both trusted Him and depended on Him, he said no.

I was so sad the day I got the divorce papers in the mail. I had told my husband he would have to go handle the paperwork, the lawyer, and the filing of the divorce…that this was his decision, not mine.

I received the papers one day when I came home from the hospital. I walked down the stairs to my cozy apartment, opened the door, and sat on the floor. The papers fell on the floor in front of me. God had already brought much healing in my heart, I had forgiven my husband, and God had worked that truth out in my feelings, but I still felt sad. I was supposed to be married. I hated the sight of those papers; they represented such pain, sadness, the breaking of a covenant before the God Whom I had come to know. But I had done everything God had asked me to do.

I had to trust God. Oh, that was so hard, and I didn't really understand what it meant. I sat on the floor and cried for two hours. I cried over what I thought could be, the life that I thought I was going to have, the children we were going to have, my childhood sweetheart whom I had known since I was fifteen. He was the sweet man who had helped me through such a hard time when my parents got divorced. I cried over the loss of a family that I had come to love. I had become so close to my husband's parents, his sister, brother, and their families; now I would lose them too. I cried until I couldn't cry anymore.

I finally got up off the floor, gathered all the papers together, and put them in a box. I had to move on; I would trust God, even though I didn't know how. I would do what was in front of me to do; I would keep saying I trusted God and see what would happen. I had come to learn that I could not make my decisions based on how I felt; I would not have gotten up in the mornings most of the time. I kept reading God's Word and made choices to obey, whether I felt like it or not. In so many things, I had seen how, in some way, my feelings would somehow eventually line up with what I was choosing to believe. I certainly didn't understand it at the time, but it was God's grace empowering me to do what I chose to believe. Philippians 2:13 says, *For it is God who is at work in you, both to will and to work for His good pleasure.*

I continued working and learning about God. I became very restless and wanted to see more of the world God created. I wanted to learn new things, I wanted to see new things, I wanted to explore. There was a lady living upstairs from me. She was a basically teacher but had become a flight attendant for one year. I asked her about it. She said, "I wanted to travel, and this was a way I could do it for a year." I thought, *Wow, can I do this? Would I leave what I went to school to do? Would I leave what I really loved to do?* I prayed about it. I talked to this lady who had been discipling me and teaching me about Jesus.

Bethany said, "Teresa, you have worked since you were fourteen, you put yourself through college in three years, you have known one man since you were fifteen, you got married when you were twenty-one, and you were on your own again at twenty-four. Maybe God wants to give you the time to grow and explore that which you didn't have when you were a teenager." I trusted Bethany. She knew and loved God and always had peace even when things did not go her way.

I prayed and asked God. I went ahead and applied for the job as a flight attendant. It had been one year since I had applied, when I drove home one day from work, checked my mailbox, and there was a letter from the airline. I couldn't believe it. Was it a refusal or an invitation? I was nervous. I waited until I got downstairs to my apartment. I threw all my stuff on the bed, sat down, and stared at the envelope. Oh, I wanted it to be an invitation. I had given up on it, actually. I had called the airline several times, and they told me if I had not heard by a certain time, I would not hear; but here was a letter!

I opened it slowly and looked inside; it was an invitation for me to come to the training! I couldn't believe it. I had sensed it was God. I had read somewhere in the Bible that all things were possible with God (Matthew 19:26); was He wanting to show me more of Himself? I had to call Bethany. She was so excited for me.

And here I was, on an airplane in the second week of my training. I was going to be a flight attendant. I was going to see the world. It might seem so simple, but I had never been anywhere, never had the desire, and thought I had life all figured out, but God said He would take me down a different path. It was starting, and I couldn't wait!

Trusting God can be scary, but trusting God is an adventure too. You are not the one controlling everything, and that can be the scary part, but I was starting something, and I knew I could not turn back.

Are you scared to trust yourself or other people or God? Read about God, about Who He is and how much He wants the very best for you. When you don't understand, you can come to a place where you know the One you trust.

Trust in the Lord with all your heart
Lean not on your own understanding
Acknowledge Him in all your ways
And He will make your paths straight.

—Proverbs 3:5–6

God Delights in Us

I had been working with the airline for five years and loved it. I only meant to work for a year, but when it came time to consider going back to nursing, I wasn't ready. I was making more money than I did as a nurse, and I loved my benefits. Traveling was amazing to me. I loved seeing the world and meeting people God had created. There was a large world out there. It wasn't just about that one little place I had grown up. Everybody did not look like me, act like me, or talk like me. People were diverse. God created us that way. Wow, I had much to learn.

At first I traveled and worked in the United States only. I had a list of places I wanted to see. Some of them were the Grand Canyon, Niagara Falls, Boston, New York, and California. I wanted to see all the national parks. I loved to hike and camp, especially when there was a chill in the air. If people didn't want to travel with me, I would travel by myself. Can you believe that a girl from a small town who had been nowhere was traveling by herself? Eventually, when people wanted to travel to different places in the airline, they would say, "Go see if Teresa is going anywhere."

I love to go to Broadway plays. We stayed in a hotel right near to where they would sell tickets in half price after 6:00 p.m. As soon as we got into our hotel, I would change clothes and rush out to see what was available. One evening I asked everyone in my crew if they wanted to go to a Broadway play with me. No one wanted to go. I rushed out on my own. Now, normally we were told not to do this, but I didn't want to just sit in the lounge and drink for the evening. They had one ticket to see *Cats*. Oh, I was so excited, but it was twenty-two blocks away. I said, "Yes, give me the ticket." I took off and had the best evening. I came out of the theater around 11:00 p.m.; I was so elated and didn't think a thing about it. I was almost dancing down the street. People were everywhere. Some guys came up and started dancing beside me. I thought they looked like lots of fun. I talked, laughed, and danced with them down the street. They followed me into the hotel. My crew was at the front desk; they saw me and came toward me. I introduced them to my friends. They had a look of horror on their faces. I wondered why. They escorted me into the hotel, but I remembered I had not said good-bye to my newfound friends. I ran back to the front lobby. They were walking out, but I ran up to them and thanked them for such a nice walk. When I returned to my crew, they lectured me for about an hour on safety.

As I look back now, I can see it was a bit foolish; my grandma always told me God took care of small children and fools. I don't think that is in the Bible, but I do believe God's grace was great with me in those days. I was a young Christian, and I believe God was taking care of me.

Another time I wanted to go to Niagara Falls, and no one wanted to go with me. One night while watching a TV program, there was a commercial about the Falls. I decided to go and so checked the availability of the flight for the next day. It was open. I was not working for a week, so the next morning, I left for Niagara Falls. I flew into Buffalo, New York, rented a car, and drove over to the Canadian side of the Falls because I had heard it was nicer. I went through immigration, which I had never done that before, and drove straight to the Falls, parked my car, got out, and walked over to the side where I could get my first look at the site. I remember my mouth falling open; they were beautiful, breathtaking. As I stood there staring, the steam going high up in the air, I saw a rainbow. Tears ran down my face; I seldom saw a rainbow for some reason. But there was one of the most beautiful ones I had ever seen. I knew it was God once more promising that He would always be with me and take care of me.

I stood there for a long time and then finally went back to my car. I had to find somewhere to stay. I drove down Niagara Parkway, saw several bed-and-breakfasts, and pulled into one. I got out and knocked on the door. A woman invited me in. As I stood there, she went back to the door and looked around. She came back in and asked where my husband was. I told her I was not married. She asked if I could possibly be there by myself. I said yes. She had a horrified look on her face. She gave me a room; I went upstairs to put everything down and came back downstairs to eat dinner. The woman, along with her husband, sat with me and wanted to know why I was traveling by myself and to tell me to be very careful. I told them I had always wanted to see Niagara Falls; no one wanted to come with me, so I came alone. When I left there a week later, we had all become good friends.

I flew into California and drove up the coast to Vancouver, stopping whenever and wherever I wanted to stop: the Redwood Forest, Columbia Gorge, the city of Seattle. It was a beautiful drive. When I arrived in Vancouver, I took a catamaran over to Victoria Island.

I flew into Boston and drove up Route 1 to Nova Scotia. I ate some of the most amazing food along the way. I stayed in a bed-and-breakfast in Kennebunkport, Maine; walked along the beach; and saw God's amazing creation. I loved the ocean. It reminded me of God's power and majesty. I thought of His grace and compared it to the waves; they always come, but we cannot control them. We can lie back on the waves and float, not knowing where we are going. We can rest in God's grace. I was learning more and more about trusting God.

I then went snow skiing in Colorado. These were some of the most beautiful mountains I had ever seen. I loved the *swish, swish,* and *swish* as I came down the mountain. And once again the mountains reminded me of the majesty of God.

Many of the flight attendants like to fly to the tropical islands on their off days. I really didn't want to go anywhere hot. It never appealed to me, but one day I told this group of girls I would go to Mexico with them. They said, "We are not going to stay in the resorts; we are going to stay right in the towns." I said OK. I knew one of the girls well; we stayed in the same room. There was one mattress on the floor, a table, sink, and small chair. That night we lay down on the mattress, huddled together. We were scared. As we lay there, we heard this rustling sound; it got louder and louder. We lighted a match. It took a few minutes for our eyes to adjust, but we saw a million lizards roaming around the room, over and around our mattress. We screamed. No one came to check on us. We eventually sat back on our mattress and stayed away all night.

The trip was OK. I had some of the best fruit I ever put in my mouth, but it was too hot for me. When I arrived home, I went upstairs to put my suitcase down. I fainted. My roommate heard the bang and came looking for me. She took me to the ER. They said I had salmonella poisoning. I have never been as sick as I was that next week.

I really didn't care for the tropical countries. I went to St. Martin and sat under a towel at the pool. It was so hot, I felt like I was in an oven. Several men came over and offered something white in a bag. I tried to make out what they were saying, but I couldn't. I shook my head no. Someone told me later it was probably drugs. What? I had led such a sheltered life.

I then traveled to Europe; I flew into London, saw the city, and then rented a car and drove through Devon and Cornwall out to the tip of England. What a beautiful site! I stayed in a bed-and-breakfast and had the best eggs, beans, bacon, tomato, mushrooms, and hot tea I have ever tasted.

I drove back around London and up to Edinburgh, Scotland. This is a beautiful city. Once I had finished there, I drove around Loch Ness to see if I could see the monster. I am pretty sure I saw it (OK, I am joking: I had grown a bit!). What a quiet, peaceful place. I drove through Wales and then took a ferry over to Ireland. Shortly after getting off the ferry in Dublin, I found myself in the middle of a riot; people throwing rocks, hitting each other with sticks, and yelling. I decided not to stay there, but I think it would have been a very pretty place to see.

Australia was one of the most beautiful places I saw. I flew from Los Angeles to Hawaii to Auckland, New Zealand, and then into Sydney, Australia. I took a ferry out into the Sydney harbor, and as I was coming back in, I stood at the side of the boat in awe. The city was beautiful, but I just couldn't believe I was standing at the side of this boat, looking at Sydney, Australia. A few years ago, I was a young girl who had been nowhere, seen nothing except for the small little town I grew up in. I could not even put gas in my car, I could not write a check, and I could not drive to the next town. This was an amazing testimony to me of God's faithfulness. He had promised He would be with me and take me down a different path. I had no idea what that would be, but here I stood looking at this breathtaking city, on a boat. My heart was filled with thankfulness. Words could not describe the way I was feeling.

I flew into Brisbane and went to the World's Fair. After a few days, I took a seaplane out to Lady Elliot's Island. I stayed in a little wooden hut, walked off the side of the island, and descended down to the Great Barrier Reef. I had learned to scuba dive a year before, off the coast of Florida, and received my certification. Can you believe that? Someone who had not been out of the city she grew up was scuba diving on the Great Barrier Reef? This was the grace and love of God; this was God showing mercy to a young girl, showing her life in a way she had never seen it and thought she never would.

The Great Barrier Reef was an awesome sight. I remember being sixty feet below the surface of the water. The sound was so muffled; it was another world down there, with another way of life. I really didn't even recognize all the things I was seeing, but God, the Creator, was showing me another part of His creation. What a gift!

I continued flying and seeing the world, but I was about to reach another decade in my life. And even after everything God had done and showed me, I started it thinking I knew what had to happen. Why did I think I had the answers now? Well, keep reading, and I will take you on another journey of my life with God.

Take a moment to just thank God that He delights in you…

Paul's prayer for the Ephesians:

> *And to know the love of Christ which surpasses knowledge,*
> *That you may be filled up to all the fullness of God. Now to*
> *Him who is able to do far more abundantly beyond all that*
> *we ask or think, according to the power that works within us.*
> *To Him be the glory in the church and in Christ Jesus to all*
> *generations forever and ever.*

—EPHESIANS 3:19–21

Hallelujah!
Sing to the Lord a new song, His praise in the assembly of the
faithful.
Let Israel be glad in its maker, the people of Zion rejoice in
their king.
Let them praise His name in dance, make music with
tambourine and lyre.
For the Lord takes delight in His people!

—Psalm 149:1–4

If you then .know how to give good gifts to your children, how
much more will your Father in heaven give good things to those
who ask Him!

—Matthew 7:11

He brought me out into a spacious place;
He rescued me because He delighted in me.

—Psalm 18:19

Relating

By now I was thirty years old, and I knew it was time to remarry. I wanted to have children, didn't I? I moved from Washington, D.C. to Lancaster, Pennsylvania. In D.C., I had lived in the big city, riding the metro and walking downtown, eating at elegant restaurants, visiting museums, going to theater, and attending parties. In Lancaster, I moved on to an Amish farm out in the country. My home was an apartment on a twenty-acre Amish farm. I had electricity, but they didn't. There were cows, chickens, and goats. The Amish worked from sunup till sundown in the fields, plowing with horses.

Why did I do this? Well, the airline was closing down the base in Washington, D.C. I had lived in the big city; now I wanted to live in the country. I wasn't ready to move back to my hometown. I still wanted to explore, see the world, but I really thought it was time to get married again. After all, thirty is getting old, right?

I had to drive down to Baltimore, Maryland, which was about an hour and a half. I didn't know anyone in Lancaster; my friends thought I was crazy and would not come all the way up to visit me. Maybe I was crazy a little. I decided the best way to meet people was to join a gym. Years later I thought why I hadn't tried to find a church.

I joined a gym that was near where I lived. I enjoyed lifting weights. On my days off, I would go to the gym every day. I was hoping to meet people. I did meet some guys and girls, and after workouts we went for coffee. They actually worked with a local airline in the city; they were pilots and flight attendants. I was not very excited about this, because I had come to see that life with the airline personnel was very transit; being in different cities, staying in a different hotel every night, and being able to do what you wanted to do gave way to being dishonest at times. I worked with lots of people who did not live by biblical principles. I was not always sure what to do with this.

But I didn't know anyone; I deserved friends, right? I remember one night standing in my apartment at the stove. My friends were coming by to get me, as we were going out. This was the first time I was going out with them other than after the gym. I didn't have a good feeling about it. I had been walking around the apartment having a conversation with God, explaining why I should go out with these people. It went along the lines of needing friends, that it wasn't good for me to be by myself all the time, that I was lonely...I could go on and on.

As I was standing at the stove, cleaning the top of it (cleaning is something I do when I am a bit anxious), I heard that voice deep in my soul, the one I had come to recognize. It said, "Don't go with this group." Oh, I knew it was God, but He was not saying what I wanted to hear. I heard them drive up and blow the horn; I stood there hesitating, and I remember saying, "God, I really want to go." I left the rag I was cleaning with, turned around, and ran out the door.

Have you ever done something and know you should not have done it? I jumped into the car that night and started laughing with them as we drove down the road. It was as if I had left God on the back burner of that stove. It was all a huge mistake. God doesn't tell us something just to give us a hard time. He knows what is best for us. He loves us and wants good things for us. I should have listened to God. If there is ever anything in my life I regret, this was it. I just said no to God or I just thought it would be OK for right now and I would come back to Him later.

Life doesn't work like that. I laughed that night. I kept talking to this new guy in the car. He was a pilot. I really didn't want to go out with a pilot. I had seen some things the pilots did, some bad decisions they made in their personal life when they were away from their families. I really knew the whole thing was wrong, but *I did it, anyway.* Why do we do that?

I did not understand at that time, that trusting God completely, in every area of life, was the best for me. You see, as I said earlier, I wanted to get married again. I wanted to settle down again, have that family, the little house with the white picket fence and two-car garage. I wanted to have children.

Relationships! I didn't understand them, and I was about to fall right back into the only way I knew to deal with them: pleasing at all cost, having an unhealthy dependency on them, looking at people (especially a man) to tell me that I was OK. Remember earlier when I said I looked to my husband to meet my needs in ways that only God could? Well, that was all I knew; I was about to look to another man to meet my needs, but God was going to show me a different way, a different path, the path He had created for me to walk on.

The young man in the car that night was a bit younger than me, and he made me laugh. When our evening was finished, he asked if he could see me again. I said yes. Before long we were seeing each other every day, and it didn't take me long to see he only wanted to have a good time. He was not interested in any committed relationship, much less marriage. I remember having that painful, wrenching feeling inside my chest again. It was similar to when my husband had left me and didn't want to be married to me any longer.

What was it? Rejection? I didn't know, but I wanted to make it feel better, and I tried the only way I knew: I tried to make him accept me, like me better, think I was good enough for him. Oh, I hated those feelings; I hated that pain in my chest, so I would try harder. I knew how to do that. I had done it before, and I could do it again…over and over, harder and harder.

There were so many times this man humiliated me, by leaving me stranded at parties while he flirted and laughed with other women. Did I tell him to stop? Did I leave him? No, what would I do? You guessed it; I would try harder to make him like me. Did God create us to be doormats? No! He created us to speak truth in love, to set healthy boundaries in our lives. We are of great worth to Him, but sometimes we are not to ourselves.

I guess I didn't know how. You see, I was too wrapped up in trying to get this person's approval, because that would say to me I was OK; it mattered *or* I thought it would.

I continued to see this man for almost two years; I was almost destroyed. I remembered those words I heard while I was standing at the stove: "Don't go, Teresa." Oh, I wished I had listened. All the wonderful years of exploring, seeing the world, traveling, and learning more about God, the world, and myself…God had taught me so much. I had not been interested in meeting anyone; I was just having fun, and I felt like it had been a gift from God. But when it came to relationships, I didn't know how to relate in a healthy way.

I was thirty, though, and thought it was time to settle down because I was getting older; but the same problems arose again with relationships. God, what was wrong with me? I kept asking Him this question. I saw myself repeating patterns over and over that were not working; I knew something was not right, and I needed God to show me truth. I was about to start down another path, a different one; I had more to learn.

Have there been times you returned to some pattern, addiction, behavior that was not good for you? Maybe because it was all you knew? God wants to show you His way, and this is how you will reach your full potential as a human being. Know Him and trust Him.

> *Don't you know that you yourselves are God's temple and*
> *that God's Spirit dwells in your midst?*

—1 Corinthians 3:16

Community of Believers

This man and I stopped seeing each other. I don't even remember what happened between us. I believe he just lost all interest and started seeing someone else. It had happened to me again—I was replaced by another woman. What was wrong with me? Was I not pretty enough? Was I too fat? After all, I was about five pounds overweight. I had always struggled with these five pounds. Is that what was wrong with me?

I kept going over and over these things in my head. I just didn't know what to do or where to turn. I had not been to church in years since my husband I had separated. The church we were going to had told me I needed to do what made my husband happy. It didn't sound right to me. They didn't have any answers for me when I needed them the most.

Remember I met Bethany and she was the one who taught me about Jesus; so I really didn't see a need to go to church. I remember after I learned about forgiveness from Bethany, I went back to the pastor to tell him about it. He listened to my story and then looked at me with such pain on his face. I will always remember his words. He said, "Teresa, I do not understand what you are talking about. I believe you are telling the truth, but I just don't get it. I could never forgive my wife if she had done to me what your husband did to you." I walked out of the church and had not stepped foot back in one.

But now I felt the need to be with other people who believed in God and believed that He made a difference in our lives. I needed to be with people who believed God was alive today, just like that scripture on the plaque behind the pastor's head read: *Jesus is the same yesterday, today, and forevermore.* I didn't know anyone like that right now. I had not seen Bethany in a long time. She lived in another state. I had been so involved with this man, but I needed more. If there was one thing I knew, I knew that.

The airline had opened a new base close to where I grew up. Was it time to move back closer to home? My family did not know God, so I knew the answer was not with them at that time, but maybe to be closer would be nice. I asked if I could be transferred. There was no problem. I moved back South. I bought a house, and everything was OK, but I knew I needed to talk with people about Jesus; where were they?

I decided I would try to find a church again, but I had no hope I would. Every Sunday I went to a different church. One Sunday morning, I walked into this church that looked like a gym. I thought, *What is this? Where do I go?* I stepped inside the door and just stopped. I couldn't see a seat; there were people everywhere. I just stood there, looked around, and finally saw the pastor standing up front on some kind of stage. I started listening to what he was saying.

He was talking about absolute truth. I couldn't move. He was talking about the things I had thought somewhere way back in my mind might be true, but I needed to hear some kind of confirmation. This man was speaking to me.

In the airline, I had seen people do just want they wanted to do. Everyone assumed they knew the truth and was never shy about giving their opinions. I didn't understand that thought process. Didn't there have to be a Creator, someone who knew how things worked the best? Didn't there have to be something for me to grab a hold of out there? Otherwise, it was just a very slippery slope. This man at the pulpit was saying there was. I was in the right place. I had found the church I was looking for.

It was hard to get involved in the church because of my schedule, but I would go at every chance I could. I was learning and hearing about God. I met some people my age, and they invited me to this singles group downtown. It was not part of the church, but many people went there, and they were all Christians. OK, I would try this.

I met the best group of single adults my age. I didn't travel as much as I did before, because I loved getting home and hanging out with these people;

I guess they grounded me. Most of the people I flew with in the airline were not Christians, and that was fine, but I just needed to hear more about God.

God had answered yet another prayer; I was going to a church that was teaching me about Jesus, that believed He was real even today and made a difference in our lives. I had found a group of people my age; we had much in common, and they all loved Jesus. I was so grateful.

God was laying the foundation. I didn't know it at the time, but He had much to show me about relationships, and the place He was going to start was with me. He needed to show me who I was by showing me who He was and what He had done for me. I knew from that time when I saw the old wooden cross on the tree that there was a purpose for me in this life, but I never knew what that was. God would show me, in His way and in His timing.

Do you have people in your life who you can be real with, tell them the truth, people who encourage, inspire, and will speak truth to you even if it might be hard to hear? If not, ask God to provide that community of believers for you.

Though one may be overpowered, two can defend themselves. A cord of three strands is not quickly broken.

—ECCLESIASTES 4:12

Serving

Solo was the name of the singles group I was attending. I had never really liked "single" groups. It had a negative connotation for me: Poor girl, she is single; can't she find someone who would have her? Why isn't she married? I felt it labeled me, and I didn't like labels. I was learning more and more as to who I was, and the last thing I wanted was to be put in some kind of a box and expected to act a certain way.

But I found such a nice group of people in Solo, and we all seemed to be on a journey with God; different places for sure, but we shared a common bond—being single. I was drawn toward them. I made some close friends there that I am still friends with today; it has truly been a gift.

There are two things that stand out to me about being part of this group, and it all centered on this particular time called Mountain Top. One Thursday night the leader started talking about an opportunity, an opportunity to serve. Maybe you cannot understand why I found this a bit weird, but I had always had so many problems of my own that I didn't have time to think about other people and their problems, their situations, their lives. What did he mean? I listened closely.

Every year Solo was involved with a mission group called Mountain Top and participated in a trip into the Appalachian Mountains to build homes for people who could not afford them. What? People in the United States didn't have homes? It was hard to believe. I became very interested in this trip. I started reading about what Jesus had to say about serving. I didn't understand, but I had this excitement stirring deep within me. How could I get excited over building a house? I certainly didn't know how, and why would I spend my time doing this? I couldn't stop thinking about it. Several of the others started talking about the trip. I asked them how they felt about it. They were not sure but had an interest. The leader planned a special meeting for all those who were interested. I couldn't wait to show up.

I went on a Saturday afternoon and didn't know any of the people. I sat down, watched, and waited. The trip was explained, all the logistics, and then we were asked who wanted to drive. Well, I didn't; it was all so new to me, and I just wanted to take it all in. One young woman offered to drive and then pointed at me and said, "I want her to ride with me." Let's just say this was one of those friends I still have today.

That was one of the most amazing things about this trip; I didn't know anyone when we started, but I became close with everyone on the trip. It was conducive to a special bond, working with people to help someone else, a closeness that is hard to describe in words.

This one man brought his tools for us to use. Now as I said, I knew absolutely nothing about building a house, but there were a few carpenters, builders, and painters with us, and they were going to teach us how. I was assigned to work with this man and all his tools. He had just bought a new electric saw to use for this trip. We were building a house for this young woman, who was two years younger than me, who had been living in her car for a couple of years. She used the cigarette lighter for electricity. Now this had been very difficult for me to comprehend. She looked just fine; her name was Franny, and I would never have thought she was living in a car. She had lost her job, couldn't find work, and had no place to live.

Well, I was told that I would put on the roof. What? It wasn't that I was afraid of heights; I had no idea how to lay a roof. Since there had to be much done before the house was ready for the roof, I helped with errands, running here and there, doing mostly what I was told. One morning the man with all the tools showed me how to use his electric saw; well, he thought he did. I watched, listened, and thought I understood. About an hour later, he was up on the side of the house and asked if I would cut him a two-by-four. I hesitated a moment but thought, *I can do this.* I went over, and guess what? I did it. Oh, I felt very good about myself. I took the two-by-four over to this gentleman and asked what was next. He told me he needed another one. I went to comply.

OK, do you understand the word "cocky"? Well, I think I got a little cocky. I went to cut the two-by-four, turned to put the wood down on the ground, and cut the cord completely. Yes, I did. It happened all so fast. I really didn't know what I had done, but everything went quiet; the saw stopped working. The man on the house looked down at me and then at the saw and back at me. I became so afraid. I knew he was going to be mad and scream at me, and I was not sure what else. As he came toward me, I believe I was literally shaking. Later he told me I had tears running down my cheeks, but I don't remember. He put his arm around me and said, "Don't be so upset; it could have happened to anyone."

Work was delayed for the next couple of hours. I was pretty shaken up and wasn't sure why. This man showed me forgiveness, and I know now it reflected the heart of Father God. I made a mistake; I didn't do it on purpose, but I always felt that I couldn't make a mistake. I had to be perfect all the time. Now who can be perfect all the time; unrealistic expectation, right? Hard to live up to, but I had always tried and got very upset with myself when I messed up. I guess I learned that somewhere early in my life, but God was showing a new way, His way, His character.

I still remember that man, what happened, and the truth I learned. It was a life-changing moment for me. I still have a hard time giving myself grace, but when I see how the God of this universe gave me grace, I am humbled.

One evening while walking around thinking about this incidence, I ran into Franny. She was standing looking at the little house that was going to be hers. I stood beside her and looked also. She turned and smiled at me. Finally she said, "I have never had a floor before." I thought I had misunderstood and asked for her to repeat what she said. She said, "When I was growing up, my family didn't have very much money." She went on to say that she had lived in a small house, and it didn't have a floor, but her mom always swept it every day and tried to keep it clean. I just stared at her. She said again, "I can't believe I am going to have a floor…"

The floor had a bit more to be done before it was finished. I told Franny that the next night at this time the floor should be completed. Let's meet at this same time and dance on the floor. She laughed and said, "I would love to do that." Then she repeated, "I can't believe I am going to live with a floor!"

The next day we continued to build the house. I had such overwhelming feelings that are hard to describe, and I had never had them before. I didn't know what they were. That evening, around the same time as the night before, Franny and I met at the house and danced on her floor. It was amazing under the moonlight, singing and dancing like a child. Franny was so happy, and I had never known such a happy feeling seeing someone else this happy.

We were dancing, singing, and laughing so loudly that we did not hear the rest of the crew come up. They watched us for a while but shortly joined us. We had such a good time; what was drawing us together like this? I believe it was the Spirit of God, His love, grace, and just the feelings that come when you reach out beyond yourself and help someone. This serving thing, I was going to have to look into it a bit more. I liked the way it made me feel inside. I didn't care that I had paid for the trip and lived in a place that had no mirror and no bathroom; this was different for me.

Little did I know that was when God may have put the spark in my heart for missions, looking out into God's world; seeing what was happening, what was going on; seeing people, cultures, and nations; and wanting to be part of what He was doing.

I came home from that trip changed; I was a different person. About eight years after this, I went on the mission field in Eastern Europe. I wrote Franny and told her what I was doing. She sent me five dollars a month for financial support for three years. This woman who lived in a car, who had never lived where there was a floor, reached out to me. Shortly after we had completed her house, she had gotten a job at a library. She wrote to me often and said she would never forget dancing on her floor in the moonlight. I would not forget, either.

I also never forgot the man who showed me God's love and forgiveness. That man who let me know it was OK to make a mistake, that I was human. This trip had truly been a mountaintop experience!

I stayed in the singles group for another year. God used it in my life. It was hard to leave, but our journey with God takes us in and out of experiences. He brings people in and out of our lives. Not holding on is hard, but the only way we continue to learn is to trust Him. God was about to take me through another life-changing experience, another mountaintop experience. Are you ready to go with me? Let's go!

God created us to love Him, others, and ourselves, and unless we function this way, we will not fully be the human beings He created us to be. Ask God to show you if you love the way you were created to.

> *Love the Lord your God with all your passion and prayer and intelligence and energy and love others as well as love yourself.*

—Mark 12:30, The Message

A Child of God

"Hi! I'm Teresa; I am a child of an alcoholic."

We went around the room; each person gave their name and repeated this phrase. I had been to several meetings similar to this one, hoping that maybe this time (please, please, please!) I would find an answer. Oh, it had been great at first. I remember, when I first read the characteristics of the children of alcoholics, I was shocked. This was the way I felt. At the meetings I met others who had been raised in homes where their needs were not met, because their parents had their own problems. Like them, I never felt like I "fit in" anywhere; I thought that was just the way it was. Needless to say, I was excited to know there were other people there who felt the same way.

At first it was helpful to sit around and talk about our problems and how miserable we were. I read every book I could get my hands on that explained why I did what I did and how I could change these behaviors. I kept trying, but every time I conquered one, another one popped up. I became very frustrated. I remember thinking, *There has got to be more than this. After all, I'm a Christian; would God really do this to me? Did God really send His Son, Jesus, to die on the cross to save me so I could be this miserable?* My only conclusion was that the best I could be was a child of an alcoholic. So I would try hard; since Jesus died for me, it was the least I could do for Him.

"Hi, I'm Teresa, how are you?"

Yes, I was attending another meeting. This one was actually for three days. At least I didn't have to tell them I was a child of an alcoholic. There was this man up front doing all the talking...such a peaceful-looking man. I imagined he'd never had any problems. Oh well, I wanted to see what his formula was.

This was two years ago, and I had given up on finding an answer. I figured I just had to accept my past; my pain and things could never change. I thought I would have to work very hard to be a Christian and accept who I was (maybe a little harder than everyone else because I was so messed up). But the very peaceful-looking man had a different story. I want to share this with you; my whole life has changed since this man told me who I am. We are free to be who God created us to be!

Genesis 1:26-27 says, *God created man in His own image.* God walked and talked with humanity in the Garden of Eden; God loved them unconditionally and accepted them. They didn't think, *Am I important? Do I matter? Who am I?* They had perfect fellowship with God.

Humanity chose to try to live without God. They thought they could do on their own. Because of their decisions, they became separated from God Who was their very source of life—identity. This was not how they were created to live. They had to attempt to gain a sense of worth and value from somewhere outside of themselves.

I remember when God showed me that my own parents had been children, and they were who they were because of what happened to them in their private world. All they wanted was to be loved just like me; I had to stop blaming them.

So we grow up believing lies about ourselves and trying to prove we are loved, accepted, valued, included, and safe, and that we belong. One of the lies I came to believe about myself was, "There is something wrong with me; I am not good enough." I wanted people to tell me differently. I wanted someone to tell me I was important, that I mattered, that I was somebody. However, the more I looked for this, the more I was disappointed. I set myself up for lots of rejection, especially with men. When men failed to tell me the things I wanted to hear, I felt rejected and believed again, "There is something wrong with me."

I remembered when I got married, I knew I had found the one person who would never reject me. This man made me feel special; I trusted him more than anyone or anything. He became life to me. Well, one day my "life" said he didn't love me anymore. I was devastated, crushed. It was like a huge bottomless hole inside me. What I thought was life left me. Since I believed that there was something wrong with me, I turned all the anger and hurt inward. I hated myself.

Now hearing this peaceful-looking man talk of God's grace and mercy, I realized that I didn't have to hate myself any longer. I didn't have to keep looking for unconditional love, acceptance, value, and worth that I yearned for so badly. The answer that I had been searching for in all the self-help books and the support groups I had been attending, God had provided. The conclusions I had come to about myself were lies. All those times when I thought, *If only I could be different, if only I could act better, if only there was a formula, maybe I could fix what was wrong with me.* God said I couldn't. God said He could. He already had. Do you realize that the moment we accept Christ, a true miracle occurs? God entered into our world, He came to us, and He rescued humanity.

We have been united with the Triune God; we are part of their relationship. The entry of Christ into you and me has given us a new eternal identity like Christ. I used to think that eternal life was something I got when I died, but God has given us eternal life right now, and this life is in His Son (1 John 5:11).

Embrace truth! Be from having to try harder yourself to become acceptable and worthy. Your past, no matter what it was, is no longer your identity. Don't accept the labels that the world would put on you; it is all they have to offer. Through Christ, God provides a way for us into His family. As God's child, you have been given a new identity and a new name. You may be thinking you do not feel anything different or act differently, but you are different. Receive from Jesus by the Holy Spirit, and He will make you whole, no longer fragmented in your thoughts, heart, mind, emotions, and body.

I know when I embraced this truth, I stopped looking to the community to tell me I was OK and I was important. Rejection still hurts, but it doesn't devastate me. Now I am free to reach out to other people, to enter into their world and reflect their Creator. This brings peace. The bottomless hole inside is gone; I do not have to perform to meet my needs. Jesus is life; I can give myself grace and received life from Him through the Holy Spirit. When I was not enough, God gave His life for me and to me so that I would be enough in Him.

Accept your identity in Christ, and be free to be all that Christ created you to be.

"Hi, I'm Teresa, a child of God!"

Grace

I like the ocean. I think it is powerful and majestic. I remember the first time I tried to float in the ocean. It was hard for me to relax; I let the water hold me up and go where the waves took me.

I looked at grace like floating in the ocean. I had always tried to control everything and everyone around me. I didn't want to get hurt or be rejected. I didn't know who I was and was always trying to prove to myself and to others that I mattered.

God has shown me who I am and Who He is. He showed me that when I was not living the way He created me to live, and didn't even know it, He entered into my world and showed what I had been blinded to. I have learned to keep my eyes on Him and trust Him. Yes, I may be rejected again, but it will not destroy me. I have learned that as I relax, I need to let go and let God be God; I can rest being His child. Life has now become an adventure! At times it feels very scary, but it truly is an adventure.

I left the internship I had taken in Atlanta, Georgia, in the summer of 1993, and started raising the finances I needed to come on staff. Talk about scary, but in January my support had been raised beyond the amount I was asked to raise.

I joined the team that was going to Budapest, Hungary, to set up the first international office. This involved selling my house and leaving my job as a nurse and a flight attendant. I had a very nice salary—scary!

I arrived in Budapest in July 1994. I left friends and family and came to a culture where I could not even speak the language. This was also very scary, but God showed me His love in a way I had never known before.

In October of that same year, God brought a man in my life whom I was only able to love because I had come to know the love of my Father. We were married in August 1995 and lived in Budapest for ten years. I had joined the organization that he was with: Youth with a Mission (YWAM).

This all sounds exciting, and it is, but it involved letting go of how I thought things ought to be. If you had asked me ten years ago if I thought I would be a missionary, I would have laughed at you. The word "missionary" scared me.

I sensed God saying during the internship, "Teresa, jump into My arms. It may not be what you always thought it would be. It may even feel like jumping into the ocean (letting go of controlling everything), but I will never let you down; I will hold you and show you many things."

It might be a bit scary, but isn't the ocean beautiful?

God's grace is beautiful.

Take a moment and thank God for His grace…

God with Me

I was sitting in a green, red, and orange room; my apartment. It was so different from anything I was used to. I was scared. I didn't recognize anything. It was all so foreign to me. I couldn't call anyone, as I didn't know anyone. Also, I couldn't go anywhere, as I didn't have a car. If I took the bus, what would I say; I couldn't communicate with the driver. Why was I here then? Had God played a trick on me?

I was in Budapest, Hungary—that is, Eastern Europe. I didn't know that a couple of years ago. I had no idea where Hungary was. I just thought "hungry" meant one thing: you wanted to eat. Seriously, my geography was bad.

I had been in this country for about two weeks. I had never felt so alone. But somehow I knew God was with me. I certainly didn't understand, but I had come a long way with God; I trusted in Him in the midst of the feelings. Maybe He had played a trick on me? Did that line up with His character? I was still learning; I didn't know.

The team of people I had come with was on the other side of the city. I didn't know what to do. I sat there with tears running down my face for a while. I am really not sure why, but I started to sing praises to God—any song I could remember about God and how great He was. I heard a ringing sound. Was that the phone? I had been told my phone was out of order and would be so for a while. I stood up and looked for the phone. I had not really been interested in where it was, because I couldn't speak to anyone, anyway. I found it, picked it up, and carefully said hello. There was much static, but after a few moments, I heard a friend from home. She yelled into the phone; it was hard to hear, but she said, "Teresa, I was thinking about you. I am praying for you. I miss you. How are you? I tried and tried to get through, couldn't, but finally I did. I love you, Teresa." I sat there crying so hard that I couldn't see. It was wonderful hearing her voice. The connection did not last long, but, oh, what a gift. I hung up the phone and continued to sing and praise God. I believed with all my heart He had just said to me that He loved me and He was with me.

Shortly after my "mountaintop" experience, God started showing me who I was in Him. He showed me who I was because of what His Son, Jesus, did on the cross. The old wooden cross I had seen years before on that tree became more of a reality for me. I started to understand exactly what happened on Calvary and what it meant for me.

I couldn't get that "mountaintop" experience out of my mind, though. The whole idea of missions was so interesting but also very scary for me. I continued to be open to what all God wanted to show me, and in the back of my mind, I remember saying to God, "If you want me to go into some kind of missions, to leave my home and family, you will have to make it so clear to me. You will have to give me the desire to do this and the desire be greater than my desire to be here, my job (I was still a flight attendant, and I loved it!), my home, and my family." Also, I liked my salary. I could do what I wanted to do and when I wanted to do it, and I didn't have to worry about money. I wasn't rich, but I had more money than I ever had before.

That had been five years before this time of sitting in the orange, green, and red apartment. Shortly after the mountaintop experience I became involved in a counseling ministry. I wanted to know and understand more and more about Jesus, God, and the Holy Spirit and how I fit into their relationship. I wanted to let go of behaviors that were hindering me in life and grab ahold of what God had for me. This took time, prayer, revelation, and patience, but over time, the desire to go out in the world and tell people about all I had learned was stronger and stronger.

I remember the first time I heard the word Hungary and it didn't mean I wanted something to eat. A friend of mine told me she was going on the "mission field" to a place called Hungary. I said, "What? Where is this…India? You can't go there. How will you do that?" She did, though, and because I could fly free with the airline, I decided I would go see her. I had started flying international, so it was not a foreign experience for me but going to

Eastern Europe was! I took her all the things I thought she would be missing. I couldn't wait to see her.

I stayed there for three weeks, and at the end of my time, I didn't want to leave. I didn't know why or how, but in some way I felt that I would be there again. I was drawn to the place and the people. I left feeling sad.

I continued to work with the counseling ministry at my church. One day the president of this ministry started telling me about taking the ministry to international level. He had a friend who was in this country with another ministry, and he was praying about going there. I looked at him and said, "You are going to Budapest, Hungary, aren't you?"

He said, "Yes, that is exactly where it is." I told him I was going with him. He just looked at me, and in my heart, I knew this was God's move and that He had been preparing the way and me.

Sometimes when I think back, maybe the whole flight-attendant experience had been about preparation: seeing the world, meeting all kinds of people, exposing me to so many different things and experiences. That little girl from that small town could not have done this; that little girl who could not write a check, could not put gas in her car or drive across town. But this woman who had been on a journey with God could, and I knew this was His plan. Now God needed to show the president of this ministry.

The time drew near, and I would need to raise financial support to live in Hungary. It was going to be for one year, but somehow I knew it would be longer for me; I couldn't put that in words, though. I did a Bible study about raising support. I had never heard of this before, and it felt very strange asking people for money to help me. The president of the ministry told me I needed to tell people what was on my heart, what God was doing, and how they could be a part of it with me. He helped me to write a letter, and I was to send it to three hundred of my closest friends. This was a very scary time for me.

I remember telling my family was the scariest thing. I knew my mom would not understand, and she didn't. She told me several years later that she didn't think it would happen, that I would never raise up the money I needed to go. I was given an amount to raise, and it came in; then the president of the mission increased the amount. He told me later that he too was very concerned about taking a single lady to Eastern Europe. God had a plan; the money came in over and beyond what I was asked to raise. Both my mother and this man could not dispute what God was doing. Mom gave her blessing to me, but I could tell she was very scared.

As I wrote my support letter, I remember thinking I should send it out to many people I had been working with at the airline. I struggled; most of these people were not Christians. They would never understand what I was doing; I was right—most did not. I had a friend who was a copilot. He was married, and both he and his wife were my friends. I sent him a support letter. I had put it in his mailbox at the airport. He got it the day he was going on a trip. He told me later that during the entire four-day trip, he talked about this letter with the captain he was flying with. He told him about this crazy thing his friend was doing and that she was saying she was going to quit flying with the airline and go to this faraway place he had never heard of before.

My friend said he had gone on like this for four days, and as they were heading back home, the captain finally spoke. He asked if he could contact me. My friend told him I was not interested in dating, that I thought I was going to be a missionary. My friend said the captain smiled and said to him, "I understand that. You see I too know this God she is serving, and I want to help her with what God is doing in her life." My friend said he just about fainted but gave him my phone number.

This man called, and we talked. I never met him personally, but this man sent me five hundred dollars and supported me financially for five years. After many years of my other friend reading newsletters and keeping up with my journey in Eastern Europe, he contacted me one day and told me he wanted to know about this Jesus. He and his wife had just had a child, and if there was a way of life he wanted for his child, it was the church.

I remember the day when I went in to tell my supervisor that I was quitting the airline and going on the mission field. He looked at me as though I was crazy. He said he had never met anyone who would leave their job, their salary, their home, their family and friends and do something like this, but he said he liked me and wished me well. It was hard to leave the airline; I loved working with them.

I sold my house, gave away everything I had, stored some things at my mom's, and left the United States. It was amazing to think that it was less than ten years before I thought life was over and I didn't want to live. It was less than ten years ago when God said, "I will take you on a different path." I was so excited flying over the ocean. I had such a passion for what I was about to do.

But now I was sitting in this apartment, scared to death. But I just had a phone call from a friend at home when I was told the phone did not work. I checked the phone again; it had no sound. God was with me. I was scared, but I knew He was with me. God, I trust you…

What is God asking you to do that you are not sure of? It may not be anything like leaving home and family, but you are still scared. Be still, and ask Him to help you be so aware of His presence and to remind you of His faithfulness.

> *He said to them, "Come after me, and I will make you fishers of men."*
>
> —Matthew 4:19

The Unknown

Those first few months living in a foreign country was difficult, exciting, adventurous, and frustrating. I remember when I first tried to use the washing machine. First of all I had never seen anything like it before. It was a little box, not anything like the one I had been using all my life. I opened it up, and there was another metal box inside the first box.

I thought, *OK, I will put my clothes in this box*. I did. Everything I owned except what was on my back. I had waited to use the machine, because I didn't know how, and now everything was dirty. I closed the first box and then the second one. There were some kind of latches to close on the outside. I wasn't sure if I had done this properly, but I proceeded ahead.

Next came trying to read the dials. I thought this couldn't be too hard—hot, cold, and so forth. Well, I couldn't make any of them out, so I just pushed a button. It took a while, but I finally figured out how to turn it on. When I did, it made a very loud noise and started jerking around; it actually moved around the tiny bathroom. I jumped back and watched. It settled but continued with the noise. I heard a water sound, thought OK, but then this rubber hose started bouncing all around the bathroom. I grabbed it and put it in the sink because water was spraying everywhere. It lay in the sink, and water ran down the drain.

I thought, *OK, it is working*. I walked out of the room for a short while but came back to check on it. The box was so hot I could not touch it; steam was actually rising up in the air. I didn't know what to do. I continued watching. The machine finally cut off. I stood there and wondered if it had finished. I left it for a few minutes because it was still so hot. When I was finally able to open the lid and touch the metal box inside, I looked at my clothes. Steam was still coming up from the clothes. They were all the same color, kind of a bland shade of blue-gray. But I had put all colors in there? What happened?

I pulled all my clothes out of the box. They had shrunk and changed colors. They looked horrible. All my nice clothes! I found out weeks later that I had one of the dials on about two hundred degrees. It had been too hot; that's why my clothes faded and shrunk. Now I had no clothes and didn't know where to go buy any.

There had been some food left in my apartment and that is what I had been eating. The dreaded time had come, though; I needed to go out of my apartment and find some food. Oh, I was not looking forward to this. How was I going to do it? I couldn't even communicate. Suppose I walked somewhere, got lost, and could not find my way back? How could I ask someone? And how was I going to buy food? I couldn't read the labels, and I didn't know how to cook anyway! All those years before when I was single, I ate out. Isn't that what all sensible, single people do?

So now not only did I have to learn how to cook but also learn how in the Hungarian language! God, this would truly be a miracle. I remember stepping out of my apartment, locking the door, and walking down the steps and outside. It was a beautiful city. I was amazed at the beauty of it.

There had to be a store close by. I walked down the street and did find a local grocery type of store. I bought all kinds of food. Some of it I recognized, some I did not. The payment process was interesting too. I had changed some money at the airport when I first arrived. I just kind of held it out to the woman and trusted her to take the right amount. I prayed God would work His miracle. He did, I guess! I had some money left over, and I had some food.

But then I had to cook it. I had never used a gas stove. One of my neighbors showed me how to light the oven. She kept talking, and I smiled but didn't understand a word she said. I watched, though, hoping I would understand.

The next evening I tried to use the stove. I did what I thought the lady had done. She told me to count to five as I held the gas button down. I did, but I always count 1,001, 1,002, 1,003, 1,004, and 1,005. I thought that is what she meant! I finished with my counting, struck the match, and *wham-bang!* The stove jumped about two feet in the air; the *bang* was so loud, it hurt my ears. Flames burst forth and spread out in my whole apartment; the neighbors came running, knocking on my door and bursting in. I stood there with no hair on my arms and no eyelashes. Do you know it takes months for your eyelashes to grow back?

People grabbed me. I guess they were asking me if I was OK; I couldn't understand them. I just stood there kind of in a shock. Once everyone realized I was OK, they left me alone. That was the hardest part. I went into my orange, red, and green living room, sat down, and cried for the hundredth time in two days. I just knew I had made a large mistake by leaving my home, friends, and family and coming to Budapest, Hungary. Many times I felt like this, but keep reading. You will see, I learned that walking down this different path with God was one of the most amazing adventures of my life.

> *Do not fear: I am with you;*
> *Do not be anxious: I am your God.*
> *I will strengthen you, I will help you*
> *I will uphold you with my victorious right hand.*

> —Isaiah 41:10

It is OK to be scared, but take a moment and realize you are not alone. Keep moving, keep walking; do what you know to do—you will come out on the other side.

> *For I will turn their mourning into joy*
> *And will comfort them and give them joy for their sorrow.*

> —Jeremiah 31:13

Marriage

The room was dark. The sun had long gone down. He just walked out the door. He kissed me on the cheek and walked out the door. I couldn't believe it. I didn't know what to do with this. I sensed the presence of God in the room with me. You know one of those times when you just can't deny it that there is someone there. It wasn't an audible voice, but I sensed these words: "Teresa, they didn't think I was the right package, either." I felt that deep in my heart.

I just sat there. I wasn't sure what to do. You see, I didn't want to get married again; or I didn't think I did. I had come on the "mission field," wanting to be another Mother Teresa; my name was Teresa, after all. In my early thirties, I wanted to get married again, and no matter how hard I had wanted to, nothing ever worked out. And then one day I just let go of it all.

It had happened one Sunday while I was walking behind this guy at church. I was following him to the sanctuary, not on purpose; we were just both walking up there at the same time. But you see I felt that strong attraction toward this man. He was the leader of the Christian singles club I had been attending. He was so handsome, and I felt that crushing feeling in my chest when I was around him.

As I was watching him, and kind of agonizing over him, I heard this voice. I had come to recognize my Father's voice, and I knew it was Him. He said, "Teresa, this is not attraction. This is craziness from your past. It is not the love I want to give to you." I stopped right where I was. I couldn't move. It all became very clear to me. This guy never gave me any attention. He never even talked to me, and I liked him! Or I thought I did. Why? I realized that this guy had never given me any attention emotionally. He even seemed emotionally distant with all women. It became clear to me. This was my earthly dad. He was not emotionally available either, never had been. I was still trying to get the love I felt like I never had, and I was trying to find it in men.

I started walking to the church. Wow, what a revelation. Right then and there I said to God that I was giving Him permission to show me the right guy and until then I was letting go completely of romantic relationships with men. I didn't understand attraction or love, for that matter, and I needed for Him to show me what it was. If God wanted me to get married again, it was His responsibility to work it out and show it all to me.

So that had been it. I had let go. Shortly after this was when I started preparing and working toward moving to Eastern Europe with a mission organization, so as far as I was concerned, God was saying I wasn't getting married again. I was really OK with it all. I had always thought I would have a son, though, and this was a bit sad for me, but I looked forward.

I moved to Budapest, Hungary. Things didn't work out exactly the way I thought. I was going to another part of the world and take the gospel. The passion of my heart was to tell people who they were because of what God had done for them. I was ready to go. God wanted to do something else.

When my team first arrived to Hungary, I ended up living on one side of the city, and the rest of team lived on the other side. I was by myself much of the time in the beginning. The two other couples were setting up house; mine was essentially set up. I waited on them, in a strange apartment, a strange city, a strange country, and a strange people. I didn't have much to do. I remember sitting one night wondering what in the world I was going to do. I was used to working, keeping very busy, but I was just walking around my apartment. I couldn't even visit with people because I couldn't speak the language. I sensed God saying to me, "Teresa, if I asked you to sit here for a whole year, do you still believe I love you? Or do you think I love you only when you are doing something for me?" I thought, *Wow, I don't know.* God wanted me to realize that my worth had absolutely nothing to do with what I did.

You see, even though I had been spending much time preparing to come to Europe, by raising support, leaving my job, selling my home, and saying good-bye to friends and family, God had been teaching me about His love and that I was valuable to Him. He had been teaching me about humanity's worth and where it came from. I realized shortly God had plans to teach me, to show me, and, yes, in the process, I may save the world! I thought, *No! I came here to tell people about Jesus; I want to do things, I want go places, and I want to talk to people.* Maybe I thought I would be important to God if I did these things? But God wanted me to know that my worth and value was not in what I did. He wanted to show me Himself.

Well, I decided, *OK, God, show yourself to me; teach me about love.* I started getting up every morning at six, sitting in a chair and waiting. I was not going to move until God showed Himself to me. I lived in an old communist apartment. This meant a high-rise apartment; I was on the eleventh floor, and I could look out the window and see several other buildings that looked just like my own. They were all very brown, dirty, and dark. It was a little scary getting up every morning before the sun came up and just sitting in my living room, but those times became precious to me. I didn't really know what it meant to "sit in His presence," but I felt like a little girl sitting in her father's lap. God showed me that I compared my earthly dad to Him. I love my earthly dad, but he didn't know Jesus and didn't have a very good childhood. He carried this over to his adult years and his fatherhood. He made promises but didn't always carry them through; he was not dependable. God gave me revelations that I thought He was the same way, that when the rubber hit the road, you might say, "I had better jump in and do it, or it wouldn't get done"; because it never did with my earthly dad. But this did not line up with God's character, and I needed to believe the truth about Him—the truth that He was showing me.

One day the leader of my team called and said we were going on a trip to Romania. I thought, *Great, now we are going to do some missionary work!* But, oh, I loved those times in the mornings with Father. I had learned to call Him that by then. I would learn more and more about what that meant as the days went by.

Now this trip to Romania was an adventure. The temperature outside was 118 degrees Fahrenheit, and I wore a pair of jeans and a white shirt. Now this is important to tell you because when I arrived in Romania after the eight-hour train ride, I was wearing dark-brown jeans, a dark-brown shirt, and my skin was brown. It was so dirty and so hot on that train. There was no air conditioner, and people were sitting everywhere—on the seats, on the floor, in the aisles, and hanging out the windows. I wasn't sure I had come to the right place.

When we arrived in Romania, we had to find a taxi to take us up the mountain to this Christian music concert that we were going to. This was not an easy task, but finally the leader of the team found one. It was very small, and there were six of us. We just stood there looking; the man was waving for us to get in. Eventually, he got a little impatient with us and pushed us into the taxi. We were mostly sitting on top of each other. Needless to say, this was a miserable ride up the mountain. The street was gravel and had many holes; the driver hit every one of them. It took about an hour to get to the concert, and when we did, the driver opened the door, and we all fell out. I was standing there dizzy, dazed, confused, and dirty. Had I come to the right place, God?

Well, that is the first time I met him. Now I vaguely remember this meeting, but he says he does. He says he knew at that moment he was going to marry me. This man was working for another mission, and his job was collecting us, taking our passports, and getting us into the concert. He introduced himself as Howard, took our passports, and left us standing for a short time. I was still trying to get my breath and wipe the dirt off my clothes, face, and hands. Howard says he was trying to figure out what to say to me. Well, he didn't choose the right words. He came back, handed me my passport, and said, "It would be a good idea for women to have their passport pictures changed more frequently. This picture doesn't even look like you." I remember turning my head around, looking up at this man, and thinking, *Who is this person? Please get out of my face.* You see, my passport picture had been of me when my hair was nice and clean, and I had makeup on. Can you imagine how I looked standing there after an eight-hour train ride in 118 degree weather and a crazy taxi ride? Well, it was probably worse than you can imagine!

The concert went on for the entire weekend. This had been a Friday, and we were not leaving until Sunday night. Saturday morning I woke up vomiting. We were staying in these little wooden huts and sleeping on wooden beds. I remember opening the door and being sick. The leader of our mission finally found some fresh water, a coke but no ice. I lay on the wooden bed until it was time to go. That was a miserable weekend. *God, am I in the right place?* I asked this question often.

Howard had been very busy the whole weekend. He said several times he wanted to find me but could not. I saw him again in a little Hungarian church. I had been in Hungary for about two months by this time and had spoken very little English if any. My team was still getting settled, and we had not been able to do much. Since they lived so far from me, I had not seen them. The service ended, and I looked up and saw this man who I recognized. Oh, I was overwhelmed; English! The service, of course, had been in Hungarian, and I had not understood a word of it. Howard saw me, and I started walking toward him. He says that at first he was a bit scared, because he realized that the comment he made to me in Romania might not have been the best thing to say to a lady. But I just wanted to speak English, so I walked straight toward him. We said hello; I then began talking, and I don't think I stopped till about four hours later. Howard had asked somewhere along the way if I wanted to go get a cup of coffee, that he knew a nice little place. He said he might have spoken about thirty-five words the whole four hours. I said good-bye to him, being so thankful for the opportunity to speak my native language; he says he had left knowing more than ever that I was the woman God had for him.

We found out that the leader of my mission and the leader of his mission were good friends and planned to work together. So Howard and I saw each other and became friends. His birthday was coming up in November. I had come to Eastern Europe in July of that same year. Howard wanted to ask me out for his birthday. He called several times, but I was busy and told him so. After the fourth time, I was able to go out with him. I was not interested in anything more than friendship, but Howard told me he was interested in more. I told him that maybe we should not see each other alone anymore. He told me that was OK; we could just be friends.

I enjoyed our friendship, and this lasted for a while. But on this night I was sitting in my apartment, Howard had told me that he loved me. He had walked me home, and I asked if he wanted to come in and have something to drink. He said yes. He said he wanted to talk to me. He told me he loved me and had loved me from the beginning. He said God had told him to pursue me and to continue to pursue me even when I said I didn't want to be pursued. Oh, this scared me to death. I told him he was too young for me, that he was from England, that I wanted to marry the "Billy Graham kind of Christian," and I told him no, no, no. He took my hand, looked me in the eyes, and told me that he was not famous, he was not rich, but we were from the most prestigious family there was…that he was a prince, and I was a princess, and he would always love me like the princess I was. Then he stood up, leaned down, and kissed me on the cheek. Then he walked out.

What? I sensed God's voice: "Teresa, people did not think I was not the right package either." I sat there for a long time. I finally went to bed. I had to travel across town the next morning to where my leader and his family were living. I was a bit nervous about traveling on the public transportation, and it was a bit far; I had to take a tram, the metro, and a bus. I had to get an early start.

But the next morning, I was only thinking of one thing: what Howard had said. I couldn't get it off my mind. I decided I would just try really hard to put it out of my mind; after all, I was going to talk to my leader, and we had much to do. I was a missionary, after all.

I walked into our meeting place, and the leader asked me what was wrong. I poured it all out to him. I had been talking and pacing the room. When I finished, I stopped and looked at him. He had tears running down his face. He said, "This man is showing you the unconditional love of God." I had a great admiration for this man and his wife. They had always reflected God's love with each other and with me. It was important to me what he had to say. What did I do with this? I said "Ohhhhhhhhh no!" and left his house.

I just started walking. I didn't want to get on a bus; I needed to get my head straight. What was going on? This was not why I sold my house and left my job, my family, and friends. This was not why I came to Budapest! What happened to being Mother Teresa? Finally I called out to God. Isn't it funny how we can carry on about something and then remember God?

I asked Him what was going on. Do you know what happened? I started remembering that time in the churchyard when I gave God permission to show me attraction, to show me love. I couldn't believe it. I sensed God saying, "Teresa, I want to give you in the physical all these things I have been showing you about love, love from Me. You told me to show you." Wow, isn't it amazing how God meets us in things, right where we are, and shows us in ways that could not be clearer? Only the Spirit of God can do this. That day, as I was headed back to my leader's house, I said to God that if this was the man He had for me, then He had to bring the feelings and show me when I saw Howard the next time. Emotions are from God, but mine had been damaged, so I did not trust them.

Well, I saw Howard about two weeks later. Can you believe he waited two weeks to call me? Howard told me later he had put it all in God's hands, and God continued to say to him to pursue me. Isn't that amazing? God keeps on pursuing us. I needed to see God's love, and He told Howard to do that one thing that I needed to see, hear, and know. God reaches down and touches the one place in our heart that needs healing. God had been showing me His love. I had needed so much healing in this place of relationships, especially with men and with marriage.

I am not sure how to explain this, but when Howard and I had spent a couple of hours together, I looked at him differently. I saw him differently. He was even cute! I knew God had given me love for this man. It wasn't that craziness that I called attraction. I didn't have to try to get this man to pay attention to me. I didn't have to beg to be noticed by him. He pursued me. He wanted me. He liked me just the way I was. This was God's love—not me trying to get his love; *he* loved me.

In January, Howard proposed to me. I said, "Ask me later."

He said, "What?"

I am not sure what happened, but I was scared. A good friend of mine was coming for a visit the next week. It was great to see her. I told her all about what had happened. She told me that I was experiencing fear, and that was not from God. We talked for a long time. I had real peace. I called Howard one night after we had finished talking. It was around two in the morning. I woke up his roommate. Howard came to the phone. I could tell he had been sleeping. I asked him if he remembered that question he asked a week ago. In a sleepy voice he said, "What question?"

I said, "Howard, wake up!" Howard told me he would ask me later.

The morning before my friend was leaving to return to the States, Howard was coming over to cook us a British breakfast. Did I tell you Howard was from England? He knocked on the door, and I answered. Howard was on one knee with a rose and asked me again to marry him. I said yes.

We were married a couple of months later at a little house on the property where my church is in the States.

I never thought I would marry a man younger than me, a man from another culture; I didn't think I would marry again at all. What I always thought was attraction was something that needed the healing hand of the Father. When Jesus came to the earth, people thought He was going to be a great mighty king, Who was going to restore Israel to a place of authority. Jesus came as a baby born in a manger. He was a mighty king, and He did restore His people to a place of authority, but, oh, it looked so different from what people thought it was going to look. Let God lead and guide you—even to that person you will spend your life with. Let God heal areas in your heart that may need healing. Maybe you don't even think you need healing. I didn't! I thought I was going to go tell everyone else how to do it, how to be a good Christian. God took me on the mission field, and he had a great work for me, but first He wanted to do a work within me. Then He wanted to participate with Howard and me to make a difference in the world around us.

Howard and I have been on the mission field for over seventeen years now, and you know what? He is still working in us, as He is working through us. Don't ever think you have it all figured out. We will continue to learn and grow; in the meantime, we can be serving in a lost world. God can do over and beyond all that you can imagine!

My beloved spoke and said to me, "Arise, my darling, my beautiful one, come with me."

—Song of Songs 2:10

Leah

My little girl, Leah…how do I tell you about her? I am sitting here asking God right now how to share with you about this precious little girl and the encounter Howard and I had with God. Howard and I had been married for about a year when I got pregnant. Now I was not going to be a young mother. Leah would be born when I was forty. Sometime this did scare me, but other times I knew it was just the right time. It was God's timing. I joked with my friends that if I had had children when I was twenty-five, they would still be in counseling. I had learned so much since I was twenty-five—so much about life, about myself, about God, and about the world around me. At thirty-nine, I just felt ready to be responsible for another human being.

We were still living in Budapest, Hungary, and at the first appointment I had with a doctor, he assumed I wanted an abortion. The doctor said I was too old to have children. When he realized that I wanted to have the child, he was shocked but did go ahead with the check-up and told me I was healthy and so was the child. Howard and I thanked him and left the office.

Howard and I were leaving for Switzerland a few weeks later. We were going to do a Discipleship Training School with YWAM in Lausanne. We were looking forward to this time.

One morning about six months into my pregnancy, I woke up and did not feel well. My legs were swollen, and I could hardly walk. I told Howard something was not right and that maybe we should see a doctor. Howard took me to a hospital. As I walked into the door, I thought I would pass out. The nurses took one look at me and helped me to a wheelchair. They immediately wheeled me to a small room.

I cannot remember too much. It is kind of like off and on things come to mind. Everyone was talking French, and they were moving very fast. I do not know what happened to my husband. Later Howard told me they came out to him and said my blood pressure was very high and that there was a chance of a stroke. They admitted me to Intensive Care.

The next three days were a blur to me. I can remember being in a bed and people doing so many things to me. I think I remember Howard's voice off and on. After three days my husband was told that if they did not take the baby, I would die and so would the baby. I had preeclampsia; my body was rejecting the pregnancy.

I remember the doctors telling me they had to take the baby, and I said, "No, you cannot. The baby is not ready." I remember Howard telling me they had to take the baby to save my life. I was so afraid.

Within twenty-four hours after the delivery of Leah, I was awake. I was more alert, but I felt so bad. My little girl was in an incubator. She was so small. She only weighed around two pounds. I couldn't hold her. She had tubes connected to every part of her body. They told Howard and me that if she lived for seventy-two hours, there was a chance she might live, but her brain was not developed, and it might bleed; if it did, there was no chance she would live.

It is hard for me to describe my feelings during that time. I was still not fully alert, I was not sure what all was going on, and I could not function properly. I couldn't think well. As I look back on this time, there are times I feel so guilty because I could not hold my little girl. I couldn't be by her side and help her; I couldn't root for her and encourage her. I have asked her to forgive me.

I was lying in my bed when a man walked into the room and told me Leah's brain had bled. It had been forty-eight hours. He assumed I would just want her discarded. I couldn't comprehend what he was saying. He thought I already knew. A nurse came running into the room and asked the man to leave. She came back, stood by my bed, reached down, and rubbed my hair; she told me again what the man had said and that she was so sorry for the way he told me. I was still not sure I understood it all.

That afternoon, Howard and I were taken into a room with a big table and about twelve people sitting around it. Someone rolled my wheelchair up to the table. A man started talking, explaining what had happened; he said they needed to take Leah off the respirator. They all seemed so hard, so cold; Howard and I both just sat there. The law in Switzerland was that they could just do it and then discard Leah, but some reason they were asking us, wanting us to understand and waiting to hear what we had to say. To this day we are not sure how this happened; they could have done what they were asking and never said a word to us. Howard and I believe it was the hand of God.

Finally Howard and I asked if they could wait and let us talk, and we would give them our decision the next morning. They agreed, which, we know today, was amazing. They did not have to do that. The leaders of the school had been with us the whole time. Staff and students had been praying. Even the international leaders of the mission had been praying for us. They were having a meeting in Hawaii and had stopped to pray for Howard, Leah, and me. That night as Howard and I lay in the bed, holding each other close, we asked Father, "What are we to do?. Do we tell the doctors to take her off the respirator? What do we do God? We cried throughout the night.

By morning we felt like we knew that we were to release Leah to Father, but first we knew that we needed to hold her, tell her how much we loved her and hand her over to Father. As we were getting ready to leave the room, the leader of the school came in with a note from the international leaders in Hawaii. Howard and I looked down and read the letter. It said, "You will know when to release Leah to Father." We walked out of the room and down the hall together. They took us into the intensive care unit and into a small room. They rolled the incubator into the room also and set Leah beside us. Before the nurse took Leah off the respirator and was going to hand her to us, she said, "Now I want you to be ready. When we remove the tube, the child will be violent; swinging her arms, kicking her feet and making all kinds of faces. Be ready." Howard and I just looked at our precious little girl. The nurse removed the tube. Leah was very still. The nurse picked Leah up and put her into my arms. She was so tiny. I held her close. Howard was leaning over my shoulder. We told Leah how much we loved her, how we wished she could stay with us, how we were going to miss her, how we wanted her, but Father in Heaven wanted to take her back with Him. Howard prayed and he cried. I have never seen my husband cry like this. I cried and I held my little girl. She felt so good. She was still breathing. After my husband finished praying, Leah took her last breath and lay very still. We felt a tremendous peace in the room, even a light; it was like God was right there, reached over and took Leah from my arms. Maybe I handed Leah to God. I couldn't get over the tremendous peace I felt. Howard said the same. I knew God was there. I knew God took my little girl. Howard and I felt the presence of God, the love of God and the peace of God. We sat there and cried. Leah was with God.

Later the leaders of the school, who was standing right outside of our door told us that the nurse who had been walking around the room, watching us, making sure everything was ok, stepped out of the room and said to them, "I don't know what is going on in there. I have never seen anything like this before. Usually the child would have been violent, but she isn't. There is something happening in there I don't understand, but I have never felt such peace."

This was one of the hardest things in my life, but it was also a time when I know that I know God was with me, with Howard and me. He took my little girl. We buried Leah's body in Switzerland. Many people have asked me why we buried her there. I am not sure I can answer that, but I know I handed Leah to God.

The mission provided a small little house where Howard and I could rest, sleep and grieve. They filled the cabinets with food and told us just to be there, not to worry about anything. I remember at one time I was concerned about something I thought I needed to do and the leader said to me, "Teresa, don't worry about anything or anyone. This is a time for you to be with your husband and just grieve because you are going to miss Leah." I look back at that and feel so thankful for her, for the mission and their provision. That is exactly what Howard and I needed. They were like Jesus to us. They could not change anything, but they comforted us, took care of us physically and allowed us to feel, grieve and just be together. That is what we needed at that time.

Howard and I had to go back to the hospital to take care of the bills. We had insurance, but for some reason, some little clause that we had missed, insurance was not going to cover Leah's hospitalization; insurance would kick in after three days, Leah lived for four days. We owed over twenty-five thousand dollars. We did not have this. I remember sitting in this office waiting for thes lady. We had been told that she needed to talk to us about the finances. I heard all they were saying, but I didn't care. It just didn't matter to me. I had just lost my daughter. I just sat there. Howard did the same.

The lady walked into the room. She sat at her desk and looked at us. She smiled and was nice. We said hello to her. She started telling us about our insurance. When she finished, Howard told her we did not have the money, we would have to pay small amounts over a period of time. I just sat there. I still didn't feel very well and I just didn't know what I could do about this money. The lady looked at me. She stared for a while and smiled at me. She stood up, said excuse me for a moment and walked out of the room. Howard and I waited. We didn't say anything to each other. We didn't know what to say.

We are not sure how long we sat there, but eventually the lady walked back into the room; she walked up to me and laid her hand on my arm. I can still remember the warmth of her hand. I can still remember the smile on her face; not a happy smile but a smile of comfort and caring. She said, "Don't worry about the money. It is taken care of." I am not sure what I said to her. I don't know what Howard said to her, either, but I can remember her face and the warmth of her hand. That was God's presence with us again; that was God's mercy and grace. God provided for us. He took care of us. I do not understand why Leah couldn't stay with us here on earth, but I do know that God was with us throughout this whole situation. He comforted us. We knew firsthand this God of comfort.

Howard and I found out many years later that the laws in Switzerland are very different than they are in the States or England. These doctors could have made their decisions and done what they wanted to do. But for some reason they made exceptions for us. Why? God was working. He was with Howard and me. He spoke to us; He gave us guidance and peace. Our little girl is with Him.

Even though I walk through the valley of the shadow of death,
I will fear no evil, for you are with me; your rod and your staff
comfort me.

—PSALM 23:4

Blessed are they who mourn, for they will be comforted.

—MATTHEW 5:4

What About Those Children?

I was standing on the side of a street in Romania, watching some children playing in the ditch. They were running around each other, laughing and playing, until people walked close by. Then they would go up with their hands open and ask for money. They were probably around the ages of four and five. I stood there for a long time, watching.

You see, I had just lost my daughter, Leah…about six weeks before. I couldn't get over these children playing in the dirt; their faces were so dirty, their clothes torn and dirty, they looked as though they had not eaten in months, and they were so young. Where were their parents? I stopped a young woman walking by to ask. She said these children were homeless; they did not have parents. My heart broke. Why, God, would you allow this? Why would you take my daughter when Howard and I only wanted to love her, tell her about You, and give her a family where she could be happy. Then You would leave children like this…children with no parents, running around the streets begging for food and money? What about these children, God?

God helped me understand. My heart was breaking. I was crying and could see nothing but these little children; the rest of the world faded away. I sensed the presence of God. I knew it was Him; there was such peace that surrounded me. I heard these words somewhere deep down in my spirit: "Teresa, Leah is with me. She is so happy, but what about these children?"

Now there was no condemnation but an overwhelming sense of responsibility, sense of compassion and love. What about those children—was He asking me? Did He want me to do something about them?

I guess somewhere deep down, I always felt like I wanted to adopt a child; even when I was very young, I would think about children who didn't have a home, didn't have parents, and wonder about them. What happened to them? Maybe somewhere I always knew I would adopt a child and give them what they needed, show them that they had a heavenly Father Who did love them and that they were special.

I continued to stand there watching the children. Howard walked up to me and asked what I was doing. I shared with him what had happened. He looked at the children; he listened and then said, "Let me pray about this." He went to his little prayer closet (that can be anywhere, even standing behind a tree!) and came back to me a few days later. He said, "Teresa, I am very open to this. Let's see what God does."

We left Romania, and I knew we would adopt; I sensed in my heart it would be a little girl. Maybe a little girl like Leah who didn't go on to be with God but was left here on this earth and would need a mom and dad. Maybe Howard didn't know completely, but I knew, and I prayed that when the time came, this little girl would run into Howard's arms, and we would both know this was the child.

What about those children? Jesus said He came to set the captive free, to rescue us from darkness and bring us into the light. What could more reflect those verses from the Bible than rescuing a child from the pit of hell? We have an enemy who wants to destroy children and never give them a chance to be all God created them to be. What can we do?

Do you have a responsibility?
What about those children?

John Luke - Light and Grace

It was one year later, on the same day of handing Leah back to God, that I found out I was pregnant again. I couldn't believe it. Since my youth, I've had a feeling that I would have a baby boy. I could even see myself playing with a little boy. He had blond hair and was so cute.

Howard and I were still working in Budapest, Hungary. I was told in Switzerland that if I got pregnant again, I would need to be very careful. Most of the time, the preeclampsia would not repeat itself, but it could. We decided I would have the baby in England. Since Leah was born the seventh month, I would go to England around my sixth month.

I was scared; would the same thing happen again? I wasn't sure I could do it again. I wanted to have this child. My husband already had a name. He hadn't even asked me. He said if it was a boy, this was the name he always wanted to name the child—John Luke. I wasn't sure. I wasn't set on any name for a boy, but John Luke? "What did it mean?" I asked Howard. He wasn't sure; he said he just liked it.

I prayed and asked God for a name, but nothing really came to my mind, so I asked about John Luke. After a while, it started to stick with me. I even started calling the baby John Luke. One day I looked up the names, one at a time. First, John; it meant God's grace. Well, I knew it would be God's grace if I would have this child. Then I looked up Luke. It meant light. Oh, I liked that; God's grace and God's light. Maybe I wanted this child to be called John Luke too—if it was a boy.

Well, I think I knew it was going to be a boy. I think I always knew. At times I would be so scared, though. What if I got preeclampsia again? What if they had to take the baby early again? I tried to put this in God's hands, but it was hard. One day I was praying and telling God how much I wanted to give it to Him, but it was hard. I turned in my Bible and found this verse in Psalms: "I will keep you in my hiding place; safe and secure." This verse was deep in my spirit; if he could keep me safe and secure, He could keep my baby too safe and secure. I started praying that God would keep John Luke in His hiding place, safe and secure.

Then I added to the prayer. As I had learned the truth about who I was—a child of God and that I was loved, accepted, and valued by God—I wanted my child to know this truth also. I wanted him to learn it a long time before I had learned it. I wanted my little boy to know it always. So I started praying for John Luke that God would keep him in His hiding place, safe and secure, knowing that he would be loved, accepted, and valued by God and that, while he is there, he will be a light that shines forth in the lives of those around him. Oh, I would cling to this verse for my child.

Well, the time came for me to go to England. I flew there, and Howard was going to join me in a month. I saw a doctor and told him my history. He could see how scared I was. He called in another doctor. This lady was so nice. I found out she was the top specialist in preeclampsia throughout all of Europe; thank you, God.

Somewhere around the middle of the sixth month, I started swelling again. Oh, the fear! In my seventh month, the doctor put me in the hospital. She did not want me to be in a room by myself, because if something happened, no one could call the doctor. I was so scared. Every day they would check the baby's heartbeat; if the heartbeat dropped, they would have to rush me to the operating room and do a C-section to save the baby.

For two months, they did this; every morning they would come in and check the baby's heartbeat and my blood pressure. Howard was with me. We both thought about Leah. We both prayed to God.

One morning the nurse came in and checked the baby's heartbeat. She worked a little longer; she started over and listened again. She left the room. I knew something was wrong; *oh, please, God, don't let it be like last time.* The nurse came back into the room with another nurse. She kept listening. She called the doctor. Within an hour I was in the operating room. Oh, it was so like before. Howard was at my head. They had to do a C-section. I just cried.

They removed John Luke from my stomach. I didn't hear anything. *Oh, please, God, let him cry.* They took him over to the baby bed and the light. After a few minutes, I heard a weak cry. They wheeled him out of the room. I screamed, "Is my baby OK?" They told Howard and me he was alive but that they had to get him to an incubator. They closed the incision in my stomach and wheeled me to the recovery room. I must have slept a bit, but when I woke up, I wanted to know where my baby was. The nurse told me he was in an incubator in the intensive-care unit for babies, but he was OK. I became very upset. I told them I wanted to hold my baby. They told me I could not at that point. I told them I wanted to *right now*. I knew it was important I hold my child, my little boy.

Finally another nurse came over because I had become very agitated. I heard her say, "Can we take her to the unit?" They took me, bed and all, to the neonatal intensive-care unit and laid John Luke on my chest. He was so small, weighing only four pounds and two ounces. I laid him on my shoulder and sang "Jesus Loves You" in his ear. I sang it over and over. I wanted him to know that he was loved. I had not been able to hold Leah until the end. John Luke needed to know he was loved, that I was there and that he would be OK.

The doctor told Howard and me that at first John Luke did not cry and was not breathing, but within seconds, he was. His blood sugar was too high, and they needed to get this in order. He said that right now John Luke was very weak, but they were waiting for him to get stronger. The doctor told us the first sign would be him crying loudly, that right now he had a very weak cry.

Howard and I spent every morning with him in the unit. One morning Howard had gotten delayed, but I wanted to go ahead to the unit to see my son. I had just gotten off the elevator and rolled onto the floor where John Luke was (I was still having to travel in a wheelchair), when I heard this loud screaming. It was a baby. It was John Luke; I just knew it was. I rolled faster and faster. I got outside of the unit and looked in. There was my baby. The nurse was sticking his heel, and he didn't like it. The nurse finished, came out, and brought John Luke to me. I held him; I could hardly hear what the nurse was saying because John Luke was crying so loud. The nurse was laughing. She said she had to stick him several times to get blood from his heel in order to check his blood sugar, and he didn't like it. We had been waiting to hear this cry; it was music to our ears. It meant he was fighting to stay alive.

The next day John Luke was ready to go home. The doctor said that was it; for about a week they were not sure which way it was going to go with him, but it was as if John Luke himself said, "Enough is enough; I want out of here!" My little boy was healthy. He was fine. He wanted to go home. He was so beautiful.

I was not too well physically, and we actually had to stay in the hospital for another week. My blood pressure remained high. Once the doctor got my blood pressure under control, she told us she did not think I should have another baby, that my liver and kidneys had been greatly affected and that next time I may not be OK. But, you know, Howard and I were OK; we knew God had another child for us, and He would bring it to us another way.

We stayed in England for two months and then we packed our car and our son and drove back to Budapest. It was a beautiful trip, the three of us, a family! I was so thankful.

Dear God, keep John Luke in your hiding place, safe and secure, knowing he is loved, accepted, and valued. And I pray he will be a light that shines forth in the lives of those around him.

Hide me in the shadow of your wings.

—Psalm 17:8

We All Matter

I was running through the streets of Budapest, Hungary. I had so much to do. Howard, John Luke, and I were leaving Europe. We were moving to a small country in Central America. It was called Costa Rica. A year ago I was not even sure where it was, but now I knew. God had given me a burden for a place I had never seen.

It had all started when someone asked Howard and me if we would help with a conference in this part of the world. I instantly said no because it was a tropical place. I didn't know much about the country, but I knew it was near the equator, and that was enough for me. Howard said he would help. Afterward I felt guilty because I did not even pray about my decision; I just didn't want to go. So I told Howard and another member of the team that I was going to pray for them, the country, the people, and the conference.

I did just that; I started praying. I had never interceded for a place or a people that much. I was not even sure how to do it, but I just started praying. I asked God how to pray. I remember one day hearing the word "foundations" in my heart. I didn't know what that meant, but the more I prayed, the heavier the burden I felt for this place. I continued to pray.

Howard told me one day that the conference had been cancelled, and they were not going to Costa Rica. I couldn't believe it. Howard and the team moved on to other projects; I couldn't. I continued to be burdened for this nation in Central America. After a couple of days, I went to the team and told them how I felt. One of the guys said, "Why don't you go there? Even without having the conference, I know this place could use help." I just looked at him. Howard didn't say anything.

A few days later, Howard came to me and said he thought I should go to Costa Rica. He had been praying about it and knew this was my strength, to go to a strange land and discern what God was saying. He said, "It is not my strength, Teresa, but I will support you in this."

I was overwhelmed. This was across the world. I couldn't leave my son and husband. Howard told me to pray about it. He said if he was not supportive of it, he could understand; but he was. Also, Howard was an excellent dad and very hands-on with our son. He was not afraid to stay and take care of John Luke. Oh, I had to pray about this; I did for weeks.

Over time, I developed a peace and desire to make this trip. We contacted the people in Costa Rica, and they were eager for me to come. We planned the trip. Howard planned fun things to do with John Luke while I was gone. They were going to have a great "dad and son" time.

I couldn't believe I was going. The moment I put my foot on the soil of Costa Rica, I knew this was the place God was calling Howard, John Luke, and me. The week was full; from the minute I stepped off the plane, there were plans for me. The eight days were a whirlwind. The people were great, and they offered us a position; I knew this was God's doing.

But what about Howard? Would he know it was God? I wasn't sure. We had just bought a house a little less than two years ago in Hungary. We had been in Eastern Europe for seven years, and we sensed God saying to "invest in the land." We met a family, and the husband was a builder. He built our house. It was beautiful. Howard and I never thought we would have a house like this on the "mission field." The family did not know Jesus, and over the two years, they had come to ask questions about what we did and who we believed in. They wanted to know more about Jesus. We were so excited for them and enjoyed getting to know them more. Was that part of the whole process of buying the house—meeting this family and telling them about their Savior? I was not sure, but I knew that Howard loved Europe (so did I), and I didn't think he would want to leave. Would he want to sell the house after only two years?

On the long plane ride home, I kept saying to God, "If this is You, You will have to tell Howard. You will have to speak to his heart; I know You would not call me somewhere without my husband. We are a family. God, I trust You."

When I got home, I was so happy to see my family. Howard and John Luke had had a special time together. They both looked very happy. Much was going on, and it was three days before Howard and I had a chance to talk. When we finally did have a cup of coffee together, just the two of us, Howard looked at me and said, "We are moving to Costa Rica, aren't we?" He told me that God had already impressed it upon his heart. I couldn't believe it. I was actually shocked to see Howard not only know this but also be excited about it all; that was only God.

This was confirmation to me. God was calling us to another land, and it all started through praying. That was amazing to me that He could put a burden on a person's heart through prayer.

We had to sell the house. I wanted to put it on the market immediately, but Howard said very clearly, "Let's put it on the market in March, and it will sell in August." I just looked at him, but he felt very strongly, so I said OK.

The house sold in August. Even though we had the house for two years only, we made money. Howard and I both had money saved in the States and in England. Shortly after we took the money from these investments, the market collapsed in the States. I would have lost the money. God guides and directs even when it comes to our finances. He shows us the way if we trust Him.

We were moving to Costa Rica. As I was running through the streets of Budapest that day, I was sad. I loved Europe; this was where I met my husband. It was where we had walked hand and hand down the wide streets along the Danube River. It was the only place my son knew. I had grown to love the people. At first this had been hard, because they were not open to new people; it took a while to get to know them, but once you did, you were their friend for life. I had friends in this city. I was going to miss Budapest.

I loved the coffee shops. I would often get out in the city and keep walking and then stop at one of the many coffee shops to either read or just watch the people. I was going to miss this so much. Maybe I didn't want to leave. As I was running through the streets, this was going through my mind. I was having a nonstop conversation with Father.

As I was running up some steps, I saw something that put it all in perspective for me. At the top of the steps, this lady was sitting on the ground with a very small child. You could see the homeless everywhere in Budapest; I am sad to say that often I would just run right past them. But this time I was compelled to stop. The lady looked up at me with pleading eyes. I felt such compassion and such pain that I soon found myself crying. I walked over and gave her some money. As I sit here writing, I can still see her face through my tears.

I realized that when we see hurting people, the forgotten ones, we see Jesus. They are everywhere, in Eastern Europe and Central America. We are called to reach out to these people and treat them the way Jesus does—with dignity and respect. We are called to tell them about the one *hope*.

At this moment was when I knew God created us all and that we all mattered. Whether we were rich or poor, like this woman and her child sitting on the ground in Budapest, or whether it was the people in Central America, wherever God called me, I would treat people with dignity and respect. I would love people with God's love, and I would share the hope I have. I was ready to go to Costa Rica.

The Adoption

"You can adopt here in this country."

What? I couldn't believe what my friend was saying. Howard and I listened intently. My friend was saying that because we own property, had our resident visas, and only had one child, we were prime candidates. My friend worked with unwed mothers and knew much about the situation with children in Costa Rica.

Howard and I had been waiting and watching in regard to adoption. We had checked in Eastern Europe and even in China. The doors had closed in Romania shortly before we inquired about adoption. With China we would have to move back to the States and live for a while; we didn't sense that was God. So we were here in Costa Rica, and honestly, I had never thought about this part of the world; could God have a child here for us?

Howard and I continued to listen to our friend closely. We had gotten our resident visas very quickly. Some people we knew had been living in Costa Rica for fifteen years and still not gotten their papers. Howard had difficulty paying so much money; he felt we were buying a child. Here in Costa Rica, my friend was saying we would just have to walk through the social system like any other person. There would be money involved but not like paying large amounts of money to authorities, governments, and orphanages. Howard and I decided we would definitely pray about this.

A few weeks later, Howard, John Luke, and I were sitting at the breakfast table, eating. We were having a party that day for children at the organization where we were working. It was one of the orphanages nearby. When we finished eating, we prayed and asked God to show us if there was a little girl for us there. John Luke was six years old. He had always been very much a part of this process. Once, when he was three years old, I was putting him to bed. As we started to pray, he asked me about children who did not have a mommy and daddy. I remember looking at him and wondering where did that come from. Howard and I had adoption on our hearts for over three years. John Luke went on to say, "Mommy, I think we should let a little girl who doesn't have a mommy and daddy come into our family. We would be a good family." Out of the mouth of a child!

Well, the day with the children was much fun, although a bit exhausting. When Howard, John Luke, and I returned home, we sat down to dinner. About halfway through our meal, John Luke said he knew which child God had for us. Howard and I looked at each other; we had actually forgotten our prayer from the morning. I asked him which one. He told us, and it took a few minutes for Howard and me to recall the particular girl. When we did, we asked John Luke why it had to be her. He said he had played with her, and she was very scared. He said he told her she didn't have to be scared, that God would take care of her. Howard and I were not sure what to say, but we thought maybe we needed to check into this girl's situation; her name was Kerry.

Howard and I started the process for adoption. Our friend took us to the social organization where we would get the application. We filled everything out, and then we had to find a social worker and a psychologist. We had some recommendations and found two ladies. First was our social worker, and the next was the psychologist.

Howard spent about two hours with the psychologist. She wanted to know everything about our life. Howard and I were not sure at first how much to talk about God but decided we would have to be ourselves and honest. We would not hold back.

I spent around four hours with the lady. After about two hours, she stopped writing and just looked at me. I remember thinking, *I hope everything is OK*. When I came to a stop, she continued looking at me. Finally she said, "I have known about Jesus Christ all my life. I am Catholic, but I do not know Him the way you and your husband know Him. Can you tell me more?" She was a dear woman, and I had several cups of coffee with her, and we talked of our life and Jesus.

This lady worked at the orphanage where Kerry was. We asked about Kerry. She invited us to come to the orphanage for a visit. The day we stopped by, there was much commotion outside of the orphanage. The psychologist was standing outside the gate to the orphanage. We asked her what was going on. She told us someone had kidnapped Kerry.

Later we found out it was her mother. Kerry mother was a drug addict. She wanted Kerry but would then get involved with drugs and leave the child on the streets with no food and no one taking care of her. This had happened again. For this reason Kerry was not declared "abandoned." This was something that needed to happen before a child could be adopted. Costa Rica would first prefer a child to be adopted by someone in the family, and they give every opportunity for this to occur. Every time the mother came back for Kerry, the judge would throw the case out and give the mother another chance. Sometime children just stay in the system, because they are never declared abandoned, and no one can adopt them. On one hand it is a good situation, because they give the mother or family every chance, but then, it is sad to see these children in the orphanages without homes.

Our paperwork was completed in a little over five months. This seemed quick to Howard and me. But little did we know that was only the beginning. So many people were standing with us. They were praying in England and the United States. We are so thankful for this prayer. You see, we completed the paperwork in May 2005, but it was August 2006 that we were declared "a family ready to adopt." We are not sure why it took so long, but we soon found out that when it came to the bureaucratic system, *everything* took a long time.

Howard, John Luke, and I had continued to spend some time with Kerry at the orphanage where she lived. We were sure this was the child God had for us. Three weeks after we were declared "a family ready to adopt," we received a phone call. It was a lady we had not talked to. She said she had a child for us asked if would like to meet her. I said, "What? Is this child Kerry?" The lady said no, that Kerry was not ready for adoption and may never be. I was overwhelmed. I wasn't sure what to do. Howard and I had been praying and giving the situation to God, praying for the people involved, the people who would be making the decisions, praying He would bring us the child He had for us. You see, we had found out that the authorities of the social system would be making the decisions about which child we would bring into our home.

Howard walked into the room, and I told him what was going on. He said, "Well, let's go meet the child."

I asked the lady when she wanted us to come, and she replied, "The next day." I just kept hearing in my head, *What about Kerry?*

We were told the next day this was just a visit. We were not to say what was going on or why we were there but just to stand off to the side and watch the child. Then we would come back to the office and talk. The lady told us this little girl was only three years old, about to turn four in a month. I remember thinking, *Whoa!* We were asking for a little girl very close to John Luke's age, but this child is so young. I felt very confused and just kept hearing, *What about Kerry?*

We drove to the orphanage. It was a Catholic home, and the nuns let us in. Children came running from everywhere. They escorted us to a room where several children were playing. One of them looked very different from the rest. She was blond with green eyes, and she was very white. Most of the Latino children were dark-skinned and had dark hair and dark eyes. Howard and I had talked much with John Luke about being an international family just like God's family—people of different skin color, eyes, and hair—and this was what I had expected. This little blond child looked just like my son did when he was smaller. *God, is this the child?*

It was the little girl they were talking about. Before I knew what was going on, the nuns brought the child up to us and handed her to Howard. I thought we were not to go up to her? The little girl hugged Howard, and Howard hugged her back. I just stood back; this was not happening the way I had thought. This little girl did not look like what I thought she would look. *God, what is going on and what about Kerry?*

The rest of the afternoon, I stood off to the side of the room, watching my husband play with this little girl. I remember just standing there trying to take it all in. One of my prayers for years had been, *God, when you have the little girl for us, I pray she will just run into Howard's arms, that Howard will be very drawn to her.* I knew in my heart that I wanted to adopt, but Howard had been the one who was not 100 percent sure, so I wanted him to be so sure, and here he was playing and hugging this little girl. She was so little; what happened to what the lady told us back at the office?

I believe we left that orphanage about six hours later. We talked with the lady and told her that we had planned to be out of the country for a few weeks, so what we should do. She told us to put something together that showed our family, and they would talk to her about us; then we could visit when we returned. Howard and I got into the car; I didn't know what to say. Howard asked me how I felt. I asked him, "What about Kerry?" He said he didn't know but that he felt very close to this little girl. I thought about my prayer for Howard and the child.

We put together a book with pictures, took it to the lady, and then left the country. I had found out later that Kerry was not declared abandoned and did not want to be adopted. She wanted her mother. The psychologist told me that she would never bond with me; she was seven years old and already had a relationship with her mother. I felt sad. That night as I was putting John Luke to bed, I asked him what he thought about Kerry. My wise son looked up at me and said, "Mommy, Kerry has a mom, and this little girl does not. She needs a mommy." I knew as I was sitting on the bed, looking and listening to this little boy, that God was speaking to me. Kerry did have a mother, and for over two years, we had been praying for her; the people in England and the States had also been praying for her. Maybe that was what it was all about—to bring Kerry and her mom back together. My heart had always been for children who were lost and did not have a home. Kerry had a mother. John Luke and I prayed for Kerry and her mom.

When we got back to Costa Rica, I found out that a family had taken Kerry into their home. It was not an adoption but a guardianship, and Kerry's mom could visit anytime she wanted. I was amazed. My question had been answered about Kerry. We inquired if there was any way we could help Kerry's mom—rehabilitation or something along these lines—but they said it was being taken care of. I stopped and thanked God. I knew we could and would not have ever been able to provide a situation like this for Kerry; we were looking for a child to come into our family and be part of our family. I thought about this other little girl.

The day after we returned from the States, we went to see "muchitata." This is what they called the little blond, green-eyed girl. Of course, it was not her name, just what they call little girls with blond hair in Costa Rica. She had another name but was never called by it. The authorities told us it would probably be about two months before we could bring her home. We would need to come by every day and visit. We took John Luke to meet her. The next day, we were coming to visit, and the nuns were standing outside with the little blond-haired girl, suitcase packed and ready to go. We stopped, got out of the car, and asked what was going on. Muchitata was ready to come with us. What? They told us it would be two months, but it had been just two days! Well, nothing had been as I had expected, so we went.

We brought her home that day. I didn't even have a bed for her to sleep in, but we put something together. That little girl slept for over fourteen hours that night, and she continued to sleep soundly for fourteen to eighteen hours a day for two months. She was very tired and undernourished.

As she was sleeping one day, Howard, John Luke, and I were praying over her. We realized that she had been born in December 2002. We came to Costa Rica in November 2002. We had been praying for our little girl for around three years, but when we arrived in Costa Rica, we prayed specifically for this child, that God would protect her, take care of her, and look after her. We found out through records that she was born on the streets at around twenty-seven weeks and had almost died. She was rushed to a hospital. Our little girl, Leah, had died when she was born at twenty-seven weeks. There were so many things that could have gone wrong with this little girl lying on the mattress, but here she was sleeping soundly in our home with us. God knew this little girl was here in Costa Rica, and she was for our family.

We closed our eyes, bowed, and thanked our heavenly Father.

We gave this little blond-haired child a new name. God adopted us into His family through Jesus and gave us a new name. We are His sons and daughters. I believe adoption is God's heart. This process took five years. I never thought it would take that long. We were told that our court date would take around three months, but it took twenty-three months. There are all kinds of stories I can tell about how our files got lost, people got sick, the social organization was raided for corruption, and our case was the only one not thrown out. I believe we were fighting an enemy who did not want this child to ever know her potential or how precious she was. An enemy who did not want this little girl to be with a family that would tell her about Jesus, a home that would encourage and nurture the gifts, talents, design, creativity, and spirit that God placed in her. I believe we have an enemy who would want to rob, kill, steal, and destroy children.

I believe we rescued this child. Thank you, God!

He predestined us to adoption as sons through Jesus Christ to
Himself,
According to the kind of intention of His will.

—Ephesians 1:5

Georgina Grace

Many people asked about the name Georgina Grace. Georgina is in honor of my dad; his name is George, and Georgina is the feminine form. Grace came from a dear prayer partner in England. She always told us Kerry was our hope. Shortly after Georgina came to live with us, she wrote and told us this little girl was our grace.

My dad was not always proud of some things that happened in his past. He still struggles with many of them. I told my dad that it doesn't matter about our past, that when we accept Jesus, we become part of a new family. When we brought Georgina into our home, we brought her into our family. We are not even sure what this little girl has experienced in her four short years, but we know a God Who is bigger than those things. We know a God Who cared for us so much that He gave His Son to die for us so that we could be reconciled with Him.

There are no second-class citizens in God's family. My dad is not a second-class citizen and neither is Georgina. Maybe the circumstances surrounding Georgina's conception was less than godly, but I believe God honors the resulting child. I believe God honors Georgina. Howard, John Luke, and I have been praying for her since before she was born. No one person falls outside of the Father's concern. Regardless of circumstances, race, gender, parentage, or performance, God is watching over every one of us, ready to respond to any who call upon His name.

Yes, Georgina is in honor of a man who has struggled most of his life feeling less. He didn't know or understand a God Who cared and loved him. But Georgina will know, and our prayer is that she will understand the power of a God Who changes even the pain of our past. I believe my dad understands this more today, and we want him to see his grandchild walk in freedom, not shame, holding her head high and saying, "Hi, my name is Georgina Grace." Grace seemed so perfect, because it is only by His grace!

Every person was lovingly and carefully formed in the womb by God Himself.

—Psalm 139:13–14

A Paradigm Shift

As I look back, I can see how far I have come on my journey with Father. I used to think being a Christian was about doing the right thing, being good enough, and trying so hard so I could go to heaven and not go to hell. I could never have told you I felt this way, but I can see it now.

Being a Christian is about living the way He created us to live with Him, participating with Him, creating and loving with Him. He had plans for the earth, and He wanted humans to be part of that; the most amazing thing is He still does!

What a different way of thinking, a different way of seeing life and understanding our purpose. Yes, God may have been angry, upset when we chose to go our own way; but I think mostly His heart was broken. He knew we would not be living the way He created us to live and our lives would not work. This broke His heart.

Wow, this is different than seeing life about trying to be good enough, trying always to do the right thing, and even seeing life as trying to "get into heaven" and "stay out of hell." As amazing as that is!

Having this paradigm shift in how I see God, myself, the world, and other people is amazing. It changes everything…such freedom! Is this the abundant life Jesus talked about?

Life is no longer about trying, striving, or wondering but about living, being present. From this place of living and being present, I am working, having a voice, standing in the authority Jesus gave me in His name, and it is about continuing to grow and learn.

It is exciting. It is adventurous. It is about being who I was all along, a human being united with the Triune God. I am free to relate to Him the way

He meant for me to. I am free to relate to the world, others, and myself the way I was meant to all along.

Salvation is not to get saved from our humanity; it is to redeem our humanity. The Christian journey is not about becoming less human, it is about becoming more fully human.

Wow, a cloud of deceit has been lifted.

The Jesus Story

Even when we did not know we needed God, didn't even know we were not living the way He created us to live, He entered into our world and came to us; He met us. We must not make ourselves immune to the suffering and pain of the world around us, but where we are, we too must enter into lives to live the life of Christ, the way He entered into our world to live the life of God.

If Jesus is God living a human life, then we have in Him the designer's blueprint for how human beings are meant to live. If our blueprint of what it is to be human is a person who entered into our world and entered into our suffering, got strung up on a cross, then we must not detach ourselves from the world.

Jesus entering into our world gives us a vision of how to be human. Any of us who have been transformed by Christ need to enter into other people's lives. When we do, the transforming story of what God does in a human heart comes alive, and the life-changing story will touch and change the lives of others too. By sharing the story of our lives, we are telling the story of Jesus.

God's method is always incarnational. He loves to take a truth and wrap it in a person.

An Elegant Overcomer

At the age of twenty-four, I thought it was the end of the world; I wanted to die. Little did I know that God was about to take me on a journey. Yes, it would be different from what I had planned; there would be pain and suffering, but it would be over and beyond anything I had imagined. It would be with God, my Creator, my Designer, the One Who was recreating me in Jesus and Whose presence was with me all the time through the power of the Holy Spirit.

These are pages from my story. As you read these defining moments in my life, maybe it will create space for you to think, reflect, be still, and listen. See if your Creator has anything to say, see if Jesus wants to share with you. I share my story only as a start to conversation; meet with people you trust, and maybe you can share and help each other. This is how we change and become the people we were created to be.

I read a verse early in my journey, which has come back to me over and over: *And if you give yourself to the hungry and satisfy the desire of the afflicted, then your light will rise in darkness and your gloom will become like midday* (Isaiah 58:10).

During a worship time just recently, someone came and prayed for me. When she had finished, she said, "Teresa, you are an elegant overcomer." She will never know what those words meant to me. I had always been afraid to be me. I had to give myself permission. I had to give myself permission to be who God created me to be. So much of my teaching had been to strive and be perfect, be someone God could love, be something different; I could be me! Such freedom! This was the abundant life I had always read about. I had to tell other people!

Arise and shine for your light has come…

—Isaiah 60:1

I am no longer a scared little girl. I am no longer a victim. I am a child of God! I am participating with Jesus with His mission in the world. And the story continues…

I will bless you who weep now, for in due time you will laugh.

—Luke 6:21

Transformational Prayers

The following are the prayers that Paul prayed for the believers. Make them personal; put your name or the names of those you are helping, and pray for spiritual formation, growth, empowerment, and being all that God created you to be.

Ephesians 1:17–23
"That the God of our Lord Jesus Christ, the Father of Glory, may give unto you the spirit of wisdom and revelation in the knowledge of Him: the eyes of your understanding being enlightened; that you may know what is the hope of His calling, and what are the riches of the glory of His inheritance in the saints.

And what is the exceeding greatness of His power toward us who believe, according to the working of His mighty power, which He wrought in Christ, when He raised him from the dead and set Him at His own right hand in the Heavenly places, far above all principality and power and might and dominion and every name that is named, not only in this world but also in that which is to come; and hath put all things under His feet, and gave Him to be the head over all things to the church, which is His body, the fullness of Him that filleth all in all."

Ephesians 3:16–21
"That He would grant you, according to the riches of His glory, to be strengthened with power through His Spirit in the inner man, so that Christ may dwell in your hearts, through faith; and that you being rooted and grounded

in love, may be able to comprehend with all the saints what is the breadth and length and height an depth, and to know the love to Christ which surpasses knowledge that you may be filled up to all the fullness of God. Now to Him who is able to do far more abundantly beyond all that we ask or think, according to the power that works within us, to Him be the glory in the church and in Christ Jesus to all generations forever and ever. Amen."

Ephesians 4:32
"Empower to be kind to one another, tender-hearted, forgiving each other, just as God in Christ also has forgiven you."

Philippians 1:9–11
"And this I pray, that your love may abound still more and more in real knowledge and all discernment, so that you may approve the things that are excellent, in order to be sincere and blameless until the day of Christ."

Philippians 2:14–16
"Do all things without grumbling or disputing; so that you will prove yourselves to be blameless and innocent, children of God above reproach in the midst of a crooked and perverse generation, among whom you appear as lights in the world, holding fast the word of life, so that in the day of Christ I will have reason to glory because I did not run in vain nor toil in vain."

Philippians 3:3b
"...putting no confidence in the flesh."

Philippians 3:13, 14
"....forgetting what lies behind and reaching forward to what lies ahead, I press on toward the goal for the prize of the upward call of God in Christ Jesus."

Philippians 4:13
{Empower them} to believe they can do ALL things through Christ.

Colossians 1:9–14

{I pray} that you would fill them with the knowledge of Your will in all spiritual wisdom and understanding, so that they will walk in a manner worthy of you, Lord, to please Him in all respects, bearing fruit in every good work, and increasing in the knowledge of God; strengthened them with all power, according to Your glorious might, for the attaining of all steadfastness and patience; joyously giving thanks to the Father, who has qualified us to share in the inheritance of the saints in Light.

Epilogue

No one escapes being wounded in this world. Those wounds do not disqualify us from being part of God's mission, but He uses our wounds to help heal those we encounter. Don't hide your wounds; when you do they become a source of shame. God's mission is not about being perfect. It is about wounded people living with Christ welcoming more wounded people into His presence.

The risen Jesus sent His followers into the world, "As the Father has sent me, so I send you." Jesus's obedience to His Father's mission cost him, we too will be wounded by this world that we have been sent to love.

Acknowledgments

There are so many people who have entered into my story along the way. It is hard to name them all; the life long friends, prayer partners, family, strangers who stepped into my life sometime for a very short time, but showed such kindness, generosity and grace. Then there are the faithful who have stayed with us for over twenty-two years and supported us financially and prayerfully as we have worked Youth With A Mission. You all have been a Godsend, His gifts – thank you.

I have read everything Shauna Niequist, Skye Jethani, N.T. Wright, David G. Benner and Henri Nouwen has written. They have contributed greatly to my own spiritual formation. If you hear their voices in these pages, it is because I know their words in my sleep. Thank you to these great authors.

There is a group of people I want to acknowledge, my master cohorts. I spent two and a half years with this community of people. We learned how to be vulnerable, real, and open. I will forever be grateful for this group of men and women.

And to the woman who had the vision for the master program since I have known her, Maureen Menard; who took the risk, didn't give up and followed her dream. You have always been a huge encouragement in my life.

A wonderful group of ladies who laughed with me, put with me, gave me great advice and just made the process of my capstone project in the masters course fun; Georgia, Anna, Simone, Ingrid, Mary, Mia, Philippi, Allison, Katie, and Elizabeth.

I am so grateful for my amazing, real, fun and loving family; my husband Howard, my son John Luke, my daughter Georgina Grace and Sir Robert, our fluffy, lovable dog. I love you and can't imagine being on this journey without you.

25815529R00068

Printed in Poland
by Amazon Fulfillment
Poland Sp. z o.o., Wrocław